My Pursuit of Praise

Pastor LaChanda Sumbler

Endorsements

In Pastor LaChanda Sumbler book she shares her own stories of abuse, heartbreak and brokenness, then takes you on a journey to healing and new life to praising God. I know her story can provide healing and hope to thousands of women around the world who are lost and hurt. I recommend you read this book and allow God to minister to you.

Joan Hunter
Author/Evangelist
www.joanhunter.org

A great book exposing witch craft and how praise really does have Power! While reading this book Pastor LaChanda Sumbler reveals many issues I dealt with that I had no idea that I could have praised my way through instead of falling back into sin or depression. The Church needs to address these mentioned issues that are right in their congregations. This is a book young adult teens as well as the more mature should read to have revelation to why their lives have been shifted Down instead of shifting Up. Thank you Pastor Sumbler! I am looking forward to the next healing book. I also was in the meeting where Joan spoke over you and prophesied you would be an Author.

Dr. Author Evangelist Sugar Trask
www.scarfree03ministries.com

Dedication

To My Son *Tyrreq Terrell Kelvon Christon*

I would like to dedicate "My Pursuit of Praise" to my Highly Anointed son Prince Tyrreq. When God gave you to me, He truly gave me a Miracle from Heaven. You are a true and perfect gift from above, and I am so honored to be your mother. Your Spirit is so strong, and I know that God has truly gifted and anointed you with a Spirit of Praise. You will go throughout the nations of the world to preach the good news of the gospel of peace. My dearest son Tyrreq, you will also continue to have and experience great victories of joy and triumph in your life. By proving yourself to be strong and proving yourself firm as you do great exploits for the Kingdom of God. May the face and the finger print of our Lord Jesus Christ shine richly upon your life always.

I Love you, Tyrreq and I am very proud of you.
Keep Praising your way through.
Isaiah 53: 3-5. You are Healed by His Stripes!
In Christ

Also, to my other son Jonathan Sumbler you have been such a joy to have in my life and to watch you grow into a wonderful young man.

Acknowledgements

I would love to send a special thanks to my father Benjamin Louis Bayone Sr., who taught me never to give up on my dreams. I know he is in Heaven rejoicing and celebrating this great victory with me. I love and miss you greatly daddy.

To my mother Rhonda Gayle Bayone, I love you so much mom! Thank you for teaching me what it means to be a woman who walks in the spirit of excellence. Thank you for teaching me to be a woman Of Godly character and integrity.

You always instructed me to dream and to dream, big!

To my siblings: Cedric Cherrie, Benjamin Jr., Keldric, Julius, Chassidy, and Joseph Bayone, thank you guys so much for always loving, supporting and making me laugh. Let us continue the family legacy. I love you guys to the moon and back, you are awesome!

Table of Contents

Introduction

There is a gift of God that is strategically located within each of Gods sons and daughters. We are all uniquely created individuals, that were created in the image and likeness of God. God wants us to know and understand that we have been supplied with His Spirit. A wonderful display of this is found in John 4:10-14, when Jesus interacted with the Samaritan woman at the well. She asked Jesus if He wanted a drink and He responded by saying, "If she only had recognized the gift that was before her, she would have asked Me for a drink instead." Her drink would have left him parch because it was temporal, what Jesus was offering was eternal. He was offering living water that was pure and satisfying from a well that would never run dry.

This authentic power source of praise is so glorious and undeniably satisfying, that as we honor Jesus who is our Living Water, He will begin to unlock hidden treasures, hidden gifts and talents, hidden potential, hidden passion, and yes even your hidden calling and purpose in life. Drinking from this spring of life given water is also a beautiful expression of praise to our Heavenly Father in the purest and most holiness form.

Psalms 22:3, tells us that God inhabits the praises of His people. What does it mean to inhabit something? It means to make your presence known; to customize it, make it your own, cause it to reflect your personality. God becomes one with His worshipers. During this season of my life I am ecstatic because I am pregnant with praise. Praise has become a part of my life line and it has provided me with a direct connection to my Father. Praise has become my source of hope, power and strength. I use praise to break forth into heavenly realms where I entertain the presence and holiness of God. Upon entering the heavenly realms, I find myself in an additive state never wanting to cease experiencing the warmth of my Fathers presence around me. My praise causes heavenly hosts to take interests and to become attracted to me because I set my mind on heavenly places. I lose myself in the love of God where I am no longer a natural being when I praise, I enter into a place where I am one spirit with God.

Praise causes us to become heroic and intelligent like the God we are praising to. God empowers us with supernatural intelligence when we enter into worship with Him. We gain revelation through the anointing of praise. You position yourself prophetically to become the very property of God. Where you are engaging in Him and He is engaging in you. The Light of God's face shines brightly on you when you praise causing Him to illuminate the dark places in your life. Heaven and Earth join forces with us when we Praise God, it's amazing how the brilliance of Heaven shines on you when you purpose in your hearts to render praise. Guilt, shame, disbelief, heartbreak, heartache, and trauma disappear when we choose to praise God. Sickness, pain and suffering must cease when true praise evokes the heavens.

During praise, we must cast our crowns at the feet of our Father. After casting our crowns, you will experience the fragrance of the Father's love. A fragrance more beautiful than any perfume or flower. A fragrance that is authentic and straight from the throne room of heaven. A fragrance to be admired and adored expressing heavenly kisses from God to the earth through our praise.

Through praise you experience the wonders of His glory and the very intelligence of God. You gain a deeper understanding of who God is. His glorious majesty impregnates us with His glorious power. His power causes scars, wounds, pain, sorrow and disappointments to leave from the core of our spirit. You then become pregnant with hope, freedom, love and purpose. Through praise we gain a better comprehension of the God-head being three, but operating in unity as one. We then enter into direct partnership with the Holy Trinity. Their matchless love encircles us and envelopes the fragrance of our praise. We impress God when we praise because that is what we were originally created for.

When we praise we join in with the heavenly orchestra and symphony that praise God throughout eternity. We join forces with His heavenly hosts, angelic beings and ministering spirits. We all join together and create a heavenly party on earth as it is in heaven. We cannot fathom in our human thinking the things that angels prevent in our lives when we praise God. Angels hearken to the voice of God and are sent to fight and to win on our behalf.

We as believers gain great territory through praise. When we praise, God enlarges our territory. Our gifts are allowed to make room for us and to place us before great men. Our gifts of the spirit operate through the leadership and guidance of the Holy Spirit. The benefits of praising God are amazing. This is a divine privilege that we should not take for granted.

Tremendous breakthroughs manifest through praise. A breakthrough of praise happens when we praise our way through a storm, through sickness, through loneliness, through fear, depression, oppression, lack, heartache, worry, guilt, shame, rejection and hopelessness.

There's a supernatural abundance of blessings and provision that happens as we praise God. The supernatural abundance is Gods supernatural, divine unmerited favor that rest on our lives. I like to call this tapping into the true richest and treasures of heaven. Once a believer hits this supernatural realm with God, his possibilities are limitless. Believers need to expose the wounds of their spirits and entertain the presence of God through Praise.

By doing this you will sense the tangible presence of God along with being lifted up as you enter into this place. The lifting up occurs when God lifts you up out of life challenges as you praise Him.

Praise is very pure, in fact it is one of the purist ways to know and experience God. In Matthew 5, Jesus said during His sermon on the Mount, *"That only the pure in heart will see God."* If you plan on seeing God then you must be willing to praise. Praise is like fire. According to Elijah it is like fire shut in your bones and it cannot be contained, it must be released. Praise can become so addictive that you desire not to keep it to yourself. You will have a praise on your lips when you wake up, throughout the day and even while you are entering into rest for the night. Can you imagine experiencing the type of praise that Paul and Silas experienced when they were bound and chained? The word of God declares that when they began to praise the jail shook and their chains were released. My God! Do you have some chains holding you right now? Does the enemy have you bound spiritually, mentally, physically or emotionally? This is your opportunity for a praise break. God is the same yesterday, today and forevermore. If He did it for Paul and Silas, He will do the same for you. Psalms 150:6

says, *"Let everything that has breath praise God."* Your current state doesn't matter to God because God can meet you right where you are when you open your mouth and begin to praise from your heart.

Praise gives you the power to overcome sadness and to experience true happiness. You become a spiritual magnet when you begin to praise, because praise is contagious. If one person is bold enough to break out in a praise, others are bound to follow. Through this book I will share with you how pursuing praise, delivered me from the Pits of my life and it will do the same for you.

LaChanda's

Pit of Pain

Chapter One

Pressed to Praise

2016 taught me the true meaning of praise. I was equipped by the Holy Spirit to defeat the enemy through praise during the darkest phases of my life. I had no clue that through my mere sacrifice, God would turn my world completely around. I never had a problem rendering praise, but during this season something changed. The praise wasn't ritualistic or coerced. I didn't have to be pumped or primed. I wanted, needed and desired something different to manifest in my life. I needed God in a way that I had never needed Him before and that was going to require doing something different on my part.

I just wasn't exactly sure at the time what that was. My life was full of despair, I was being abused mentally, verbally, emotionally, spiritually, financially and yes even, psychically. I found myself living in Hell on earth with no way of escape for myself or my son. Everything around me made me feel as if I was being controlled by unseen forces. The word says we wrestle not against flesh and blood but principalities in dark places. Well, they had it out for me and it appeared that they were winning. My life was being controlled, my decisions were being controlled and my destiny and purpose were being controlled by forces outside of myself. I personally believe it was the spirit of witchcraft, which is a force to be reckoned with. Witchcraft is a very manipulating spirit that comes to destroy the Christian mind, body, soul and spirit. This demonic force has no respect of person because it doesn't care what your race or financial background is. It doesn't care who your parents are. It doesn't care anything about you. According to John 10:10 it comes to STEAL, KILL and to DESTROY and witchcraft is one of the tactics that is used.

Witchcraft will rob you of your joy, your, peace, your smile, your health, your wealth, your integrity, your character, your destiny, your purpose, and the call of God on your life. This spirit will get into your mind and have you contemplating suicidal thoughts. You will find yourself plotting evil against others. This spirit of witchcraft is very dangerous and there are a number of people who have no idea that they are being controlled by this spirit. They have no clue that they have been exposed and infected and that healing must take place. Many believers attend the house of God Wednesday after Wednesday and Sunday after Sunday never realizing that they are an easy target for this destructive spirit. We pay our tithes, worship, dance and sing praises unto God, but leave the sanctuary to return to a life filled with dysfunction. We find many ways to mask our inner battles and struggles. We deal with addictions and bad habits that we cannot seem to break. We stay in ungodly and unhealthy relationships. We find ourselves indulging in adulterous relationships or overcome with lustful spirits that lead to fornication. God's chosen elect find themselves in sticky situations that are unseemly and have no clue how they even found themselves there.

Again, the spirit of witchcraft is deceptive and very strong, to the point of having you to deceive yourself and thinking that you can deceive God. We seek and search for breakthroughs in our lives, but they seem few and far away. We look for God to open new doors, but as soon as the door opens it appears that it quickly shuts. Nothing that we do seems to prosper. Nothing that we touch turns to gold, it turns to sand in the midst of our hands. When seeds should be manifesting blossoming flowers, they produce weeds. As a believer, this is heartbreaking because you know that you love God and you know that your desire is to please Him, but things are not going according to plan.

These are the thoughts that were running rampart through my mind because I love God and I have done my best to serve Him with my life. Yet, I have not seen many favorable days. From a dysfunctional childhood to a failed marriage, my soul was a target for the enemy and he was trying to destroy me by any means necessary. I entered a very abusive relationship that could have cost me and my son our lives, BUT GOD! This gentleman was a distraction that was being controlled by the spirit of witchcraft. He was a ploy in the enemy's plan to destroy my life. The enemy wanted to paralyze me and stunt my growth and he had me for a while, but God is a deliver. I didn't know how to deliver myself, but God did. My life had been predestined before the beginning of time and no matter what, I have to live out each day, moment and hour o my life. We have no idea what each day entails, which is why we must trust God and trust the process.

Many of us are fighting wars that we had no business entering into in the first place. Therefore, we are fighting with the wrong strategies because many have no idea what we are fighting against. We have not taken the time to identify the true enemy. We are walking onto the battlefield blindsided without the proper protective gear. We are not fighting with our spiritual weapons provided for us by God. The bible says in Ephesians chapter 6 to put on the full armor of

God. The key word is FULL, because you have no idea where the enemy is going to attack. At any given moment, he can attack your mind, which is why you need the helmet of salvation. You don't know if he is going to attack your heart, which is why you need the breastplate of righteousness. The ultimate goal is to be ready when the enemy attacks. I had to learn this first hand.

I can recall growing up and being violated by my mother's brother. This man who was supposed to be my uncle, molested me. Can you imagine the agony, the disgrace and pain that I felt as a young girl? The fear and torment that I battled with for years. The daily visuals of this man doing things to me that shouldn't be done to a little girl. Having to see him around the house or at family functions and to act as if nothing ever happened. This was not a one-time event. This went on well into my teenage years and I did not tell a soul. I was 38 years old when I finally told my parents.

Yes, 38 years I lived with this pain in my soul. I lived with a hole in my heart. There was a part of me that was missing, that had been stolen by this infiltrator. He was sent by the enemy to destroy my life. But I thank God for His word that says, "ALL things work together for the good of those of who love the Lord and who are called according to His purpose." Well, I know that I have been called to advance the Kingdom of God through evangelism. I am convinced that the sorrows I have experienced were for the glory of God. Did they feel good while I was going through the sorrows, of course not, but today I understand the bigger picture.

Therefore, I am compelled to tell my story. My story is someone else's story because there is nothing new under the sun. I am an overcomer and God is allowing me to share my journey so that others can overcome as well. There is freedom and liberty where the spirit of God is, but the spirit of witchcraft will have you chained and bound. This is not the will of God for our lives. He did not provide the gift of Jesus Christ for us to remain in bondage. He provided the gift of salvation for us to open and use to our advantage.

The spirit of witchcraft and any other force from the pits of hell has already been defeated. The time has come for us to rise and to declare that we are the righteousness of Christ. The power of darkness shall not prevail. Praise is a POWERFUL weapon and throughout this book we are going to learn how to use it to defeat the enemy.

In Gods eyes you are simply beautiful in every way. It doesn't matter what others say because God is the author, finisher and creator of our faith. This is why we should praise God no matter what. He sees us in our purest and rarest forms. He looks pass our faults and short comings and He sees our needs. He looks pass our sinful nature because of the blood of Jesus and His love covers every sin that we perform knowingly and unknowingly. There are many who have never been told that they were beautiful or special. Today I would like to tell you straight from heaven that you are loved by God without condition. We do not need man's affirmation.

Allow Jesus the lover of your soul to search the hidden treasures of your heart and birth out your true beauty. A beauty that will be gloriously appealing, joyously given, and amazingly cherished by everyone you encounter. This is the true beauty of praise. A praise that will cause you to press pass the pressure and trust in a living of.

A praise and confidence that even on the roughest of days you will still lift your holy hands. Thanking the God who made you. Thanking Jesus for making you beautiful and filling your heart with praise.

Chapter Two

All in God's Plan

I was Born to two amazing parents, Benjamin Bayone Sr, who has gone on to be with The Lord, and my mother Rhonda Bayone, in whom I treasure dearly. My parents were very good parents, my father worked very hard, while my mother stayed home to raise my six siblings and myself. Growing up as a child I experienced many bouts with asthma, sinus and pneumonia. I recall waking up many mornings struggling to breath, while wheezing due to the asthma. Even though I loved school, my random bouts of illness caused me to miss many days. I was the only girl in the family for many years and I grew up with three highly energetic brothers, whom I adored. I had siblings to keep me company and entertained, but for some strange reason I always felt isolated and alone. I knew that there was something different about me, but I didn't know what it was.

As a typical young girl growing up I was often misunderstood and rejected by many, but today I understand that this was normal for children. I found comfort like most little girls in playing with my Barbie dolls. On a beautiful sunny day, I would find myself in a mystical land of fantasy with me and my dolls playing doll house. I loved playing outside, experiencing the beauty of Gods creations, but I had limited access because I was the only girl. My mother didn't want me outside doing what my brothers were doing, being typical boys.

Being at home was one element of excitement for me, but I had something altogether different to face when I attended school. I loved attending school, but I faced many challenges due to my learning disability which caused me to be placed in special education classes. This was a difficult time for me because I just wanted to be normal like my peers. This was not a part of Gods plan. Jeremiah 29:11 says, God knows the plans He has for us. Apparently these challenges had a purpose, but I had to stay the course to find out what the purpose was. It was a challenge trying to learn at the level of my peers, but I couldn't and this made me very sad. I struggled so much in school because children don't care that you have a disability. I was teased and mocked by my peers because of the thick glasses that I wore. I was born legally blind in my left eye and partially blind in my right. Can you imagine the constant taunting of being called four-eyed? If that wasn't enough the teacher gave me a hard time as well. She would often belittle me and tell me I wasn't going to make it in life. I was a child and had no idea why this person who was supposed to encourage me felt the need to speak discord into my life. This caused me much grief and despair. I would often find myself crying and feeling alone and isolated. The kids were one thing, but this was an adult I was supposed to trust. The enemy had it out for me and he was willing to use those I trusted to created wounds that would create an early pit of despair.

Rejection caused me to become a little girl that would shy away from others. I found myself running from my peers, instead of developing relationships because I didn't want to be talked about. This was a lonely place to be in, but I developed protective barriers at an early age. I mean no one wants to feel pain, we will seek to avoid it at all costs. When I think back over my life I understand that there were some other missing factors in my life. I hear women today talk about being a "daddy's girl" but I have no clue what that looks or feels like. My father was present in my life, but he worked very hard. He was always absent from the home due his job. I didn't have the leisure of running to his arms and getting the reassurance that I was beautiful and not to concern myself with what others thought. I didn't have the pleasure of him looking deep into my soul and reassuring me that I could do all things through Christ who strengthens me.

I began battling with rejection at a very early age. I was left alone to deal with the wounds that were being developed in my heart. I was left to my own thoughts and understanding of who I was based on what others said. The words of others began to shape my thoughts of who I was. I began to believe what my teacher and my peers said about me. My father's absence spoke very loudly in my life.

Growing up I also enjoyed riding my bike and watching my favorite cartoons. I also loved to dance. Oh, how I loved to twirl around the room and get lost in motion. I had an uncle named Fred who taught a dance class. This gave me an opportunity to be around other young girls in a different setting. I was also surrounded by family members who were in the class as well.

2nd Samuel 6:14, declares, "David danced before The Lord with all his might, and David was girded with a linen ephod."

Like David, dancing was a way of expression for me. This was a true gift from God that seemed to take me into a different realm. I was extremely talented, so much so, that my mother entered me in various dance recitals. I would wake up on Saturday mornings, overjoyed about the recitals and how beautiful I would look after my mother dressed me. I always felt like a princess dancing solo or in front of hundreds of people with my group. Dancing made me feel normal. I didn't feel like the little girl that my peers and my teacher tried to portray me as.

At that time in my life I found comfort in making people smile, laugh, clap and praise God. I believe that I was in preparation for my future. I was being prepped on how to press pass the crowds, get lost in God and stand on a platform designed for His glory. There was greatness on the inside of me, but the enemy was trying to block me from seeing it based on what others said. I now know that God was pruning me for leadership. I was being taught at an early age how to overcome adversity, rejection and isolation because these are things you experience when you have been called to ministry.

What I love about God is that these things didn't just pop up, they were predestined for my life. Sure, I would have chosen not to have a disability. I would have desired to be in regular classes and not have to wear thick-glasses. It was all going to make sense one day. Romans 8:28, assures us, *"[with great confidence] that God [who is deeply concerned about us] causes all things to work together [as a plan] for good for those who love God, to those who are called according to His plan and purpose."*

As I stated I was very isolated with the exception of being around my cousins. I didn't have to really deal with them teasing me as much. I possessed a very quiet spirit and my mother would often remind me of my purpose in life. I did my best to never trouble my mother, I focused on being a good girl. I was engulfed with the peace of God at a very early age. I didn't quite understand it at that time, but I fully understand today that the spirit of God was with me. The spirit of God was empowering me to stand against the wiles of the devil.

And all your spiritual children shall be disciples taught by The Lord and obedient to His will, and great shall be the peace and undisturbed composure of your children. Isaiah 54:13

I was being taught by the Lord to do His will, I just didn't know it at the time. I enjoyed spending time with my father. My little eyes would light up like headlights on a car when he walked through the door from work. I couldn't wait to jump in his lap and tell him about the events of my day. Unfortunately, this wouldn't always happen as I expected. I loved my parents, but we didn't have a healthy home life. I experienced living in a broken home that was full of dysfunction. As a child, I didn't understand mind altering substances, but my father would often drink when he returned from work. He battled with alcoholism, which caused him to transform into this person that I didn't like.

If you know anything about alcoholism, you know that it is often coupled with abuse. I grew up witnessing my mother encounter abuse at the hands of my drunken father. To see my mother cry dug a deeper hole in my already wounded soul. I had no idea that what I would see as a little girl, would one day become a preview of my future. We often shy away from what we see and tell ourselves that will never be our story. Yet, somehow, we end up experiencing the same foolishness. This curse found its way into my future.

I might have been legally blind, but God gifted me not to be spiritually blind. I was blessed by God to see into the spirit realm at a very early age. I would witness the unseen forces that dominated the life of my father in a very horrific manner. I was terribly afraid of him as a little girl, but God always sent His angels to minister to me and to teach me not to fear.

For he will give his angels a special charge over you to accompany and defend and preserve you in all your ways of obedience and service. Psalms 91:11

Due to my father's battle with alcohol I wasn't as protected as I should have been as a little girl. My father did offshore work which caused him to be gone for weeks at a time. During his absence, I would spend time at my grannie's house, hanging out with one of my relatives. This was a critical time in my life because I was developing into a pre-teen. There were several things I hadn't learned about myself and I was already in a fragile state because of my disabilities and home life. One thing I have learned about the enemy is that he does not stop strategizing and creating ways to destroy our purpose.

I enjoyed visiting my grannies house because it gave me an opportunity to escape the dysfunction of my home. What I didn't realize is that dysfunction can follow you anywhere because it is a spirit. I left my home of alcoholism and abuse to find myself being violated by my uncle. Yes, my uncle was molesting me. He would gain my trust and then lure me to a secret place, where he would attempt to assure me that he was not going to hurt me. Then he would touch me inappropriately, putting his hands over my mouth and bidding me not to scream or say a word. I can't tell you how I felt the first time this happened. I didn't fully understand it all, but I knew that he was not supposed to be doing it. I was lost in the moment because this was worse than the kids taunting me or the teacher mocking me. Maybe she was right in her assumption, that I wouldn't do anything in life. Being molested by my uncle took me into a dark space. This was not a one-time incident; this brutal act went on until I was fourteen years old. This hurt me to the core. Each time I would cry and literally find a place to go to in my mind until he finished. Despite it all, I knew that God was with me. My heart shattered and quite naturally fear set in. Here I am afraid of my father and now this. I didn't tell a soul about this until the tender age of 38. All those years I held on to this dirty secret because I was afraid and I was ashamed. Even though I was the victim, it was very embarrassing. Not having that fatherly assurance and protection in my life, didn't give me the confidence I needed to confide in him at the time. Even though my father had been delivered from alcohol around the time that the abuse stopped I still didn't feel safe. I carried this pain for years. I was unravelling and no one could understand why. My soul was vexed and tormented. I couldn't look at myself or be alone without seeing him or feeling him touching me. I had to suffer in silence with just me and God. He took my innocence without any remorse. I was told to shut up and take it, even though I expressed the pain and discomfort. This caused me to be jumpy and suspicious of all people. My level of trusting boys was at a bare minimum because I had been traumatized. I was empty with no understanding of how to be refilled. My life had been truly interrupted by these events. My self-esteem and self-image were very low. I felt dirty because I was carrying this secret that I couldn't share with anyone. My perception of life was very cloudy at this time and I had become a slave to my thoughts and to my pain. They were controlling my life in the worse way. I didn't care about life anymore. I just wanted it all to be over. I wanted the feelings and the visions to stop. I was lost and I was sure that I would never be found.

As I grew into a young woman I didn't have an eye for picking the right male companion. I viewed them all the same. They had a motive and more than likely would end up violating me or not protecting me because that is what I was used to. I found myself doing some of the many things that people do when they are broken. Getting involved with the wrong crowd, turning to drugs, alcohol, sex, dropping out of school and some even turn to the same sex for comfort. Not because they want to, but as a coping mechanism or bandage for their bleeding soul. A bleeding soul that leaves you helpless and lifeless. You become like the walking dead, just existing and not living. You appear dead, therefore everything you touch has no life. No matter what you do things can't seem to come together.

Only God has the power to deliver you from satanic attacks such as these. I thank God today that He preserved my soul for such a time as this. I had to encounter this violation, to come out victorious and to share with others that God is real. Like Job, I believe his strong mantra, *"Though you slay me, yet will I trust you. Job 13:15"*

Chapter Three

A Miracle in The Making

Have you ever been in a place of desperation? I have often heard people say that desperate times call for desperate measures.

I left my parent's house, got married and became pregnant. We were blessed with a son named Tyrreq, who was born with a complexity of health issues. He was born very premature and spent the first four months of his life in the NICU. Can you imagine carrying a child for nine months with a wealth of expectations? Yet, when they are born you have no clue whether they are going to live or die. Each moment is critical. Every breath Tyrreq took could have been his last. Can you imagine the place of desperation I was in at that time? If I didn't know God, this was a testing point to see just how strong my faith really was.

I recall meeting with the doctor at the Rapides Women's and Children's Hospital. He came into the room and what he had to say totally shifted my life within a matter of seconds. He explained to me that Tyrreq was a special needs baby with an unidentified syndrome that would leave him battling with sickness for the duration of his life. He went on to say that Tyrreq would develop several diseases leaving him chronically ill. I didn't fully understand all that the doctor was saying. I believe I went into a state of shock. I began to ask the doctor what could have caused this to happen to my baby. He went on to explain that I have a byconner uterus which means it is made in a heart shape and is split down the middle. Therefore, becoming pregnant meant that Tyrreq grew only on one side of the uterus, causing him not to fully develop. I wasn't quite six months pregnant when my water broke. He is my miracle child because he was born with underdeveloped lungs. He was born with six fingers on one hand, requiring him to undergo the removal of an additional thumb through surgery in his first month.

He was very difficult to feed and kept colic. Reaching developmental growth milestones was very difficult and slow for him. As a mother this was very difficult for me, but I understand that God will not put more on us than we can bare. Therefore, I had to be able to handle it, if God allowed it.

After it was all said and done, Tyrreq was diagnosed with:

- Mild Mental Retardation

- Mild MRI

- Scoliosis

- Chronic Asthma

- Chronic Allergies

- Chronic Sinuses

- Slow Growth Syndrome

- Headaches

- Pancreatic Insufficiency

- GERD

- Onychomycosis

- Eczema

- A Topic Dermatitis

- Tinea Vision

- Speech Delay

- Food Allergies

He had to receive Occupational, Physical and Speech therapy. My life was no longer my own, because I had been given a huge task to care for this precious vessel that God entrusted to me. It takes a special person to sacrifice their life for another human being. I know beyond a shadow of a doubt that God chose me for this assignment. I could have been angry with God, but I chose to trust Him with all of my heart, my mind and my soul. I love everything about my son and I have learned so much about God, life and love through watching him. He has been a true joy and an inspiration because of the image of Christ that is displayed through his life every day.

I remember bringing Tyrreq home with very special instructions on how to care for him. This was going to require a lot of work and for the average young mother it would have more than likely been overwhelming. I would often worry that he wouldn't live through all that his body was enduring. With the underdevelopment of his lungs the doctors assured me that he wouldn't live pass five years. That is what they thought, but God had something else in mind. God had anointed me and given me a special divine assignment from Heaven to care for His son, His Prophet, Tyrreq.

God had given me His grace to let go of my wants, needs, dreams and desires to care for Tyrreq's wants, needs, dreams and desires. Let me clarify that this journey has not been easy, but God never promised us easy, He promised us victory. I could not image my life without him, I simply would be lost, Tyrreq is the best thing that has happened to me. He is my world and I know that I am his world as well. When you see me, you see him we are always together. He is my perfect little angel, that lights up my life day by day.

Since Tyrreq's birth he has undergone several surgeries, been on several oral medications and shots to control some of his symptoms. He has encountered several doctors and specialists who to this day still have no clue what his true condition is. Yet, God knows and He has a perfect plan for it all because all things work together for the good of those who love God and who are called according to His purpose. One thing is for certain both I and Tyrreq love God, so He has to show up according to His word.

I can already say that Tyrreq has defied the odds because there is, so much the doctors said he wouldn't do and today he is able to do. If I had to do it all over again, I would. I can honestly say it cost me a lot. The sacrifice has been great. The days and nights of not sleeping because I had to administer breathing treatments. Having to pray for temperatures to break and administering meds in the middle of the night. There were nights I would hold him in my arms praying in the Holy Ghost from 1:00am to 5:00am and sometimes longer. The doctors made it very clear that he needed his breathing treatments in the wee hours of the morning and I was willing to sacrifice sleep for him to live. This wasn't about Tyrreq being my son, but more than anything it was the fact that he was important to God and I had been given stewardship over him. This made the difference in how I showed up for my son.

I would often speak healing scriptures out loud over Tyrreq and this would bring him and I great comfort and much needed peace. I made it my business to surround him and his room with nothing but the Word of God along with Praise and Worship music. I did not allow certain people or things around Tyrreq, because he didn't like a lot of noise. The most amazing thing about Tyrreq and me caring for him is that when Tyrreq would be sick in the hospital for days and weeks at a time we would feel the presence of God and the closeness and nearness of Jesus in a very special way.

In the midst of having to travel from state to state seeing different specialists the glory of God was always near and this is why I Praise Him!

I hold Jeremiah 30:17 near to my heart, "But I will restore you to health and heal your wounds declares the Lord, because you are called an outcast. Zion for whom no one cares."

I truly believe that God is going to heal Tyrreq and fully restore his life. I can honestly say that through his life he has been very positive, maintaining a heart of gratitude.

It doesn't matter how hard the storms of sickness has been in our lives I will continue to rejoice and praise God. We know that Jesus is a Healer, and Tyrreq will receive a cure for the type of unknown syndrome he has, even if it's a Praise Cure!! Hallelujah! To God be the Glory and the Praise!!

Chapter Four

The Unexpected Storm

"When He got into the boat, His disciples followed Him. And suddenly a violent storm arose on the sea, so that the boat was being covered by the waves; but Jesus was sleeping. And the disciples went and woke Him, saying, "Lord, save us, we are going to die!" He said to them, "Why are you afraid, you men of little faith?" Then He got up and rebuked the winds and the sea, and there was [at once] a great and wonderful calm [a perfect peacefulness]. The men wondered in amazement, saying, "What kind of man is this, that even the winds and the sea obey Him?" Matthew 8:23-27, Amplified Version

The weather warns us when storms are going to arise in various parts of the country. One thing I have learned about the storms or life, they come with no warning. They show up and have the potential to destroy your entire life. I am a living witness because I had to bear a storm that shook me to my core and that changed the trajectory of my life.

I can recall a beautiful sunny morning where I would get up and do my morning ritual of getting prepared for work. Before going to work my husband and I would have to drop Tyrreq off at my mother-in-law's house. I would inform my husband of my work and class schedule so that he would know what time to pick me up. This particular morning my husband was acting pretty strange and I knew that something wasn't right. He dropped me and Tyrreq off and went about his day so I thought. When I arrived I found that my scheduled changed and instead of calling my husband I caught a ride home with one of my classmates. During this time, I couldn't drive. I would normally stop and pick up Tyrreq, but on this day, I decided not to. I kept sensing that something just wasn't right. I got out of the car and thanked my classmate for the ride. I proceeded into the house with the expectation of unwinding from the day. As I was walking through the house

I noticed a bright red pager on the stereo speaker. Back then pagers were popular and as I stood there I began to look at the numbers. I stumbled upon a number that looked very familiar to me and because I was curious and concerned I called the number and a man answered the phone. I said, "Hello I have a red pager with your number on it, did you by any chance leave your pager at my house?" The man said, "No I did not" and he began to cry and say that the pager belonged to his wife. He went on to say, "I had been wanting to tell you that our spouses have been secretly seeing each other for a while now." He began to break down the details and I was speechless. He said they would sneak away often by lying about their work schedules. I stood there cold and lifeless, while the anger in his voice penetrated through my soul. We hung up and he immediately came to my house to pick up the pager and he looked me dead in my eyes and said he was going to kill my husband. This left me feeling very angry, confused and scared all at the same time, I simply didn't know what to do.

Suddenly I heard a still small voice tell me to be still, vengeance belonged to Him. This was truly an unexpected storm because my husband had been cheating on me for months and maybe even years. Not only was he cheating on me but it was with another man's wife. At this point I was deeply troubled. My husband returned home and I confronted him and like most men he denied that anything ever happened. I knew he wasn't being truthful with me. As the days and weeks went on, he finally confessed that it was true, that he indeed was having an affair and not just with one woman. He is currently married to the woman he was cheating with. What I love about God is He made the lady who had been cheating with my husband, in our home apologize to me. She has since given her heart to the Lord, and she came to me like a real woman. She said she was sorry for breaking up my home, because she knew how much I loved my family. At that moment, I had to make a conscious decision to either give her a piece of my mind, or stay in peace, forgive her and let her go. I chose the high way. I chose to look her dead in the eyes and tell her, I forgive you! At that moment, I realized how powerful forgiveness can be. I released her and let her go by forgiving her and this was not only for her, but for me as well.

Often, we as believers and even non-believers endure the storms of life, and for me this was a storm that I wasn't expecting. This was an intense storm that blocked my view and destroyed everything within its path. It wreaked havoc on my life in a major way. Every facet of my life was affected. When it's storming outside, there is always great darkness, the sky turns gray, the clouds become dark, there's often lots of rain and lighting. Depending on how fierce the storm is sometimes it may be multiple storms going on at one time. From all the turbulence that the storm is bringing, you look and think, will this storm ever cease. Will things ever be normal again?

If you are experiencing a storm right now, do not fret because it doesn't last forever, it must pass. Your storm may the same as mine, dealing with an unfaithful spouse or a sick loved one. Your storm may be financial, mental or your children could be getting out of hand. You might be a single parent with no idea how to provide for your family. People experience different types of storms every day. Some are hail storms and some turn into tornadoes. Our human nature is to become afraid of things that we have no control over. They cause us to become timid and fragile. We must know that the same way that Jesus spoke to the storms and told them to cease, we have that same power according to our faith.

Prophetic Utterance: The Storm

As your Lord and Savior, I want you to realize that there is not a storm in your life or life's circumstances that I your Lord cannot and will not handle. I am the Storm in the Middle of the Storm and my power is all sufficient, all powerful, all glorious and never ending. I your Lord am so powerful that even the toughest hurricane will never come against my great power. The revelation to the beautiful passage of scripture is majestically great because I am the creator of the winds and the sea. I was there before it all began. I was ever present as a master builder when it all took place, you see what I want my children to realize is I am in the midst and in control of it all. Nothing surprises me that has happened, will happen, and is about to happen in your life. The good news is you're not left alone in the storms of life, I Am the Storm in the middle of the Storm. As my children, my prayer is that you will begin to live care free, by trusting completely in Me and My ability to bring you completely out of the storm, with the full assurance of faith that I am in the middle of the storm with you. This is my ultimate promise to you! Be Still and Know that I am God! If the storm is cancer I am there. If the storm is marriage related I am there. If the storm is business related I assure you I am there as well. If the storm is financial failure I too will be there. Begin to thank Me for My peace in the middle of the storm.

Chapter Five

A Storm Within the Storm

a ban doned

ə'band(ə)nd/Submit

adjective

1.having been deserted or cast off.

synonyms: deserted, forsaken, cast aside/off; jilted, stranded, rejected; informal dumped, ditched

Being abandoned leaves an individual feeling broken, lonely, afraid, rejected and deserted. I had experienced this feeling many times in my life. From my father not being there, having to hide the violations from my uncle and even caring for my sick child. I had my moments of abandonment but when I met my husband I just knew that I would never have to experience that feeling again. I felt that I had found my safe place. I left my parent's home, married my husband and set off to have a blissful life. It started out great, but somewhere along the journey things took a drastic turn. After finding the beeper and my husband adulterous confession, our relationship went south. The storms of my life escalated into a hurricane and I was experiencing a storm within a storm.

I can recall the night he announced that he was leaving. He looked at me with no remorse and said he was sending me back to my parent's house. He declared that night that he was not helping me with anything else. I felt so depressed and confused. I was extremely afraid and worried because he was the sole bread winner. How was I going to take care of a special needs child with no income? I tossed and turned that entire night thinking how was I going to make it? I would still attempt to reach out to him for assistance. Every time he would say, "I am not giving you a dime" and "Stop calling me and asking for money." Then he would hang up the phone in my face. As a woman, this hurt me to the core of my very being. I didn't understand for the life of me what I could have done for him to treat me so awful. As the mother of his child you would think I would have been worthy of more respect. I began to question myself as a woman. Was there something wrong with me? Was it my weight? Was I no longer pretty enough? Could it have been my cooking, my cleaning or my love making? Did I not serve him as a friend, companion or great listener? What did I do wrong?

I loved him and I thought he loved me, but how could he hurt me like this. How could you give someone your heart and they just stump all over it? We shared so many intimate things and intimate moments and for it to come to a place of bitterness and disgust was unreal. I would find myself questioning his motives over and over again. The enemy found an entry point into my soul when this happened, because it shifted my perception of myself as woman. I began to believe the negative thoughts that I projected based on my ex-husbands abandonment. The little worth that I had left after my tainted past was now depleted. He made it very clear that he was done and my biggest fear of starting over was a present reality. I had no idea how I was going to make it without him. What was my life going to look like as a divorced woman with a special needs son? The reality of being a single mother began to sink in and it was scary, but I knew that the same God who kept me with my son, would keep me through this as well.

When you pass through the waters, I will be with you, and through the rivers, they will not overwhelm you. When you walk through the fire you will not be burned or scorched, nor will the flame kindle upon. Isaiah 43:2

My dear friend we all go through something in life. Your trial, might not be my trial and vice versa. You may be crying wondering how you are going to feed your kids. You might be battling with an abusive mate and need a way of escape. You can find yourself crying in the night, but you have to know that joy will and can come in the morning. Pain and heartache has a way of crippling you, only if you let it. The lies of the enemy will have you lost and shielding yourself from society. It will cause you to lose your identity and some attempt to find it in other people, places, drugs and alcohol. Pain has the potential to blind you, causing you to lose sight of your God given purpose and destiny. You will begin to question Gods love for you, because you feel alone, broken and bruised with scattered thoughts. You know that God sees all and He knows all, but you can't help but wonder if He is watching the suffering you are enduring.

I remember screaming to the top of my lungs to the Lord saying, "I can't do this My Lord." In a sweet, still small voice, He replied, "Yes, you can make it My Daughter. With me your Lord and Savior by your side you can do anything. My Grace is sufficient and My strength is made perfect in your weakness. You will overcome this, and you will make it my child."

I knew that God was with me, but my spirit was truly crushed. My heart felt as if it had been shattered into a million pieces. Then to top it all off he continued to be nasty and arrogant towards my and his son. I held Psalms 34:18 near to my heart which says, "The Lord is near to those who have a broken heart, and saves such as have a contrite spirit."

I can recall a beautiful sunny day, Tyrreq and I had just left church and we would take a ride after church, which became our Sunday ritual. We enjoyed riding around the town and checking out the scenery. On this particular day, I decided to travel down a road that I had never traveled before. It is safe to assume that I should have maintained my normal route. I just happened to glance to the right and spot my soon to be ex-husbands vehicle. As I continued looking my ex came out of the laundry mat with his new girlfriend. My flesh immediately rose up and took over. I turned into the parking lot, jumped out of the car and World War 3 erupted between the two of us. I could barely get the words out as I yelled to him, "This is what you left me for?" He had nothing to say as he and his girlfriend jumped into his car, leaving me standing there as if he never had a wife or a son.

I was already hurt, but seeing him with this woman caused me to become devastated.

I believe this day was the day I truly experienced the difference between heartbreak and heartache. As a woman it hurts you to know that the man you once gave your heart to is with another, but it becomes heartache when you actually see them together.

My feelings after seeing them together, was first total shock and disbelief but reality all at the same time. It felt as though someone had literally taken a knife and stabbed me in my heart. When Tyrreq and I arrived back home I found myself bent over the toilet vomiting up my guts for the remainder of that day. I was left with a huge whole in my heart and nothing to fill it with but God. That is what I love about God. When we face betrayal, He is there to pick up the pieces of our heart.

In the darkest hour of our lives, Jesus reaches out His hand so gently and sweetly and looks at us through His eyes of love and compassion and says, "I Am He" and " I Am Here" for you.

The "Great I Am" is present and will be present in this season of life for you. He loved me right out of this time and season of grief, defeat, fear, loneliness, confusion, sadness, and brokenness. He gave me an inner strength, peace, joy and ability I had never experienced before. It was His presence in and upon me that carried me through one of the darkest hours of my life. He did a work in me that caused me to smile when I should have still been crying. According to Psalm 16:11, *"You will show me the path of life; in your presence is fullness of joy, at your right hand there are pleasures forevermore.* I was able to find joy in the presence of God and the anointing made the difference in my life.

Chapter Six

The Romancer of My Soul

The experience of seeing my ex-husband with his mistress caused fear to grip my soul. The days, weeks and months following that experience caused me to realize the I was now alone. The person that I looked to for comfort, outside of God was no longer present and I found myself wondering who was going to fill this void. Who was going to love me, hold me, care for me, dry my tears and ease my pain? How would I find joy in such a lonely place? What or who would cause me to smile again? My life as I envisioned had been stolen from me and I desperately needed to find myself. I needed the inner strength to move on with my life and to live again. I began to dream about being swept off my feet by this perfect gentleman. Have you ever heard the statement that the "Holy Spirit" is a gentleman? I heard it many times, but never had the experience of meeting the Holy Spirit on the level that I was about to.

God had a plan, a plan that would completely sweep me off my feet. It all began during a Sunday morning service. I was so excited and full of complete anticipation about meeting Jesus. Any other Sunday I would awaken out of my beauty sleep, and prepare myself for Sunday morning worship service. Like most women I would prepare my Sunday best outfit. On this particular Sunday I felt different, I felt alive, as if I was preparing for something supernatural to occur. For this first time in years I felt like a princess, beautifully dressed and adored, and ready to meet the lover of my soul, Jesus. I arrived at church and during worship I experienced the undeniable love and presence of God. I had not experienced the presence of God to this degree since the beginning of my heart break with my ex-spouse. My Lord and Savior Jesus stepped into my life and my current situation and He began to shower me with His presence. I was draped with a supernatural overwhelming presence of His agape love for me. The richness of His love was truly mesmerizing and breathtaking. His presence was peaceful, pleasant, tangible, and very beautiful. As I laid prostrate before heaven the love of my Father engulfed me. I showed up expecting something new and fresh from my Father and I received my heart's desire. My Father met me in my dry place and became the romancer of my soul. No man could have done it better! After being romanced by the Holy Spirit, I could never settle for anything less. From that Sunday, I knew that I would never be the same and that what I needed only God could provide. Anything from man would be extra.

In love, we partake of His life and live in Christ. Hosea 2:7 says, "And she will pursue her lovers, but will not overtake them, and she will seek them but not find them, and she will say I will go, and return to my first husband, for it was better for me then than now."

God had a very special plan for me that day. He illuminated my inner man and caused me to experience the love of Christ for myself. This love supersedes anything that you have lost. This love will give you a peace that surpasses all understanding. This love will replace the love that you did not receive from those who you wanted to love you. Those who didn't understand your value or worth! This love will provide joy and freedom, because whom the Son sets free, is free indeed and we were set free because of His unconditional love.

You too can experience the fullness and richness of God's love. He is simply beautiful in every way imaginable. He is ready and willing to be the romancer of your soul.

That you may really come to know practically, through experience for yourselves, the love of Christ, which surpasses mere knowledge without experience, that you may be filled through all your being unto all the fullness of God, may have the richest measure of the divine Presence, and become a body wholly filled and flooded with God Himself. Ephesians 3:19, Amplified Version

Chapter Seven

Tyrreq's Butterfly Kisses

God is mindful of His children and very gentle and kind. Children carry these same attributes because they see through innocent eyes. They don't judge or point fingers, they simply love no matter what. They don't see color or gender, they just see love. In my darkest hours, when life seemed to suck the literal breath out of my body, my son would make his appearance. When I contemplated giving up and throwing in the towel, Tyrreq would come into my room. He would crawl his little self into my bed, wipe my hair away from my forehead and gently kiss me. Today I understand that through my sweet son, God was affirming His love for me. Throughout the day, my son would walk around and blow me kisses and tell me, "catch mommy." My son would notice bushes of flowers and he would always pick the prettiest ones and he would run towards me with a smile on his face and say, "mommy these are for you." During this time, I felt pain like never before, but God through Tyrreq didn't allow me to wallow in it.

God was using my precious son to assure me of His infinite never ending and never changing love for us. Every time I felt the urge to quit I would look at my son, and would realize there is a God in Heaven who is looking out for the both of us. He was empowering me not to quit on Him or my son, and as a mother Tyrreq was worth the fight. God through my son, lit an inner fire in me to begin to take charge of my own life. I began to make life happen for us and it was simply amazing how God began to repair and restore my life. The enemy spoke and said I would have to return to my parents' home. God had another plan for me and my son, I was blessed to get a job at the same school my son went to. My landlord went down on my rent which was extremely high for a single mother. I bought my first car before I even obtained a driver's license. I purchased new furniture for our apartment, and God superseded all this when the divorce was final with a generous amount of child support and alimony.

My life was turning around quickly and I was truly beginning to see the hand of God on my life. He made a way for us where it seemed to be no way. God had truly proven himself to be faithful toward us. At this point, all I wanted was my Father.

God was gentle and blowing me butterfly kisses through the power of His presence, and He had begun to create a holy righteousness in me.

Do not earnestly remember the former things, neither consider the things of old. Behold I am doing a new thing! Now it springs forth, do you not perceive and know it, and will you not give heed to it, I will even make a way in the wilderness and rivers in the desert. Isaiah 43; 18-19

As you are reading this, I don't know what you are going through, but God knows and He is saying that you can make it! He is with you every step of the way. When others fail you, God will not fail. When others let you go, He will never forsake you.

God will deliver you with His righteous right hand. God says, "Do no fear, for He is God."

Fear not, there is nothing to fear, for I am with you, do not look around in terror and be dismayed, for I am your God. I will strengthen and harden you to difficulties, yes I will help you, yes, I will hold you up and retain you with my victorious right hand of rightness and justice. Isaiah 41: 10

The Lord is always present to walk us through and strengthen us during the most difficult seasons of our life. He makes a remarkable promise with one word found in this passage of scripture, and that word is " Yes" I will help you.

I would say to you in this hour in your life, to nullify the "no" in your spirit, and begin to put a Yes Lord in your Spirit. Jesus said that all His promises are, "Yes and Amen." Begin to tell God yes and watch God begin to turn things around for you and your family. Let Him surround you with butterfly kisses of His promises. Begin to give Him a heart pounding Yes God from your lips! Let Him hear you say,

"Hallelujah! Yes, to your will Lord; Hallelujah Yes, to your way Lord!

Not long after my ex-husband and I had separated I began to get heavily involved in church. I was attending church on a regular basis, going to life groups on a weekly basis, and serving in the choir where I first learned about worship. I had also began serving by teaching in the children's church, being a greeter and attending prayer during the week from 8:00-10:00am. The church was well disciplined in prayer especially praying in the spirit. My pastor would often say, you cannot deal with life naturally speaking without the infilling of the Holy Spirit. He would often say if you don't pray in the Holy Spirit the devil will think he is winning. The interesting thing that blew my mind about praying in the Holy Spirit is found in Romans 8: 26-27, *"In the same way the Spirit [comes to us and] helps us in our weakness. We do not know what prayer to offer or how to offer it as we should, but the Spirit Himself [knows our need and at the right time] intercedes on our behalf with sighs and groanings too deep for words. And He who searches the hearts knows what the mind of the Spirit is, because the Spirit intercedes [before God] on behalf of [a]God's people in accordance with God's will."*

I was growing spiritually, but I still had to deal with life here on the earth. Learning how to pray in the spirit brought me great joy and peace. When I was facing the most difficult time in my life, the Lord blessed me and Tyrreq with our first car. My brother Keldric, took me on Hwy 71 where there were no cars and taught me how to drive. I had my car for a little over a year when things really started getting tough for me as a single parent and I could barely pay my car note. My son Tyrreq was always sick which caused me to miss a lot of work to stay home and care for him. This caused my pay check to be short and I didn't have enough money to cover all my bills. The car dealership would call and threaten to take my only form of transportation because I was three months behind on making a payment.

I remember the day like it was yesterday, it was on a Saturday and they said they would pick my car up that Monday morning. I remember weeping bitterly before the Lord asking what shall I do? I had no other source of financial assistance, and the Holy Spirit instructed me to get in my car and drive around my neighborhood and pray in the Holy Spirit. I did as the Holy Spirit instructed me and I drove around my neighborhood praying in the Holy Spirit and thanking the Almighty God for keeping Tyrreq and I with transportation. I noticed as I was driving and praying in the spirit, I could sense the nearness of the sweet presence of God. God was assuring me that He was in the midst of us and that it was His will for us to have a car to drive. I began to cry even harder because the presence of God was so sweet upon me, to the point that it was captivating. As a result of me obeying the voice of the Lord through the power and presence of the Holy Spirit that dwells within me, that Monday morning the car dealership called and said they would not come and get my car. They decided to decrease my monthly payments and give me time to catch up no matter how long it took, as a result of this I was able to keep my car, and that's was the onset of my willingness to praise a mighty God.

Chapter Eight

The Sun Will Shine Again

"Arise from the depression and prostration in which circumstances have kept you, rise to a new life! Shine be radiant with the glory of The Lord, for your light has come, and glory of The Lord has risen upon you, For behold, darkness shall cover the earth, and dense darkness all peoples, but The Lord shall arise upon you O Jerusalem, and His glory shall been seen on you, and nations shall come to your light, and kings to the brightness of your rising." Isaiah 60:1-3, Amplified Version

There are times in life when it appears that there is no way to escape disaster, hurt, pain and suffering. Times when we can't see our way or find a way of escape. We find ourselves sinking low into a pit of depression and despair and feel that life is not worth living. We experience dark thoughts of throwing in the towel and thinking that death would be easier than living life. The enemy tries to convince us that ending our life wouldn't matter because no one would miss us anyway. We reach the bottom of the barrel with no energy and thoughts of how to get back to the top. How do we escape these pits of life? How does things get better?

Is there a Kinsman Redeemer? Is there one we can acquaint with and fully understand and know my pain or a spirit of heaviness that I have carried far too long? Yes, my dear sisters and brothers, there is a Kinsman Redeemer and His name is Jesus Christ. In this hour, He would commission you to ARISE from your place of despair. Arise from depression! Arise from fear! Arise from oppression! Arise from lack! Arise from peer pressure! Arise from low self-esteem! Arise from rejection! Arise from past mistakes! Arise from alcohol and drug abuse! Arise from guilt and shame! This is your time to ARISE for the Light has come!

Jesus who is the Light, will give you the strength and courage to ARISE, by his Power and Glory resting upon you. This is your opportunity to RISE to a new life in Christ, a new place of peace, joy and love through the Holy Spirit. You will experience His grace, mercy and freedom from a place of despair and a sinful nature.

At one point in my life I was struggling really bad and I just wanted to be accepted and to have someone in my life. God was doing a work in my life, but I had to allow God to renew my mind so that my body, heart and soul could fall in line as well. I was still battling in my flesh because on Friday's and Saturday's I would get dressed up and go out to party and have fun. My friends would tell me I read the bible too much. They said I was too young to be that serious about God. They tried to convince me to lighten up and have some fun.

Little did I know because my mind was not yet renewed, I yielded to the lies of the enemy and worked during the weekdays, partied on Friday's or Saturday's and went to church on Sunday's. This was a big no, no from God! I still had my sin nature but the power of the Holy Spirit would begin to convict me every time I entered the club. I must be honest and admit that majority of the time I would override his ruling and his unction. Even though I tried to avoid the voice of God His grace would still abound in my life. I finally came to a place in my life where I realized that I didn't need what the world was offering. All I needed was God. It got so bad that I would find myself coming home crying after partying, it wasn't fun anymore. I understand today that God wanted me, but the enemy wanted me to so I was in a tug-of-war and quite naturally God won. Matthew 6:24 says, *"No one can serve two masters; for either he will hate the one and love the other, or he will be devoted to the one and despise the other. You cannot serve God and mammon [money, possessions, fame, status, or whatever is valued more than the Lord]."* I had to make a choice and eventually I chose the One who first chose me.

Chapter Nine

Riding the Waves

In 2016, I was caught off guard by another storm called "sickness" and the doctors had no idea what was wrong with me. I had to stay in the hospital for several days and no matter how many tests they ran, they could not get an accurate diagnosis. I was told by several different doctors I had blood clots and an irregular heartbeat. I was losing weight rapidly and I could barely walk or talk. I was in constant pain and I kept a headache, a backache and my blood pressure continued to drop. At any given moment of the day or night it would drop below 80 or just into the 70's. I was very weak and tired and I couldn't drive or feed myself. I needed assistance getting in and out of the tub and getting dressed. I had to be transported to the hospital via ambulance to receive IV fluids due to dehydration and feebleness. I lost all my hair as a result of this sickness and the test I took demanded that I get stuck with a needle to receive strong medication via IV to run test. My veins where bruised and blown because I was getting stuck repeatedly.

One day during my stay in the hospital the doctors discovered endometriosis, an enlarged cist, tumors that looked cancerous and an enlarged uterus with scarring in my tissue. This was causing excruciating pelvic pain and the only solution to the problem was a full hysterectomy.

This was another storm that I was not prepared for. Up to this point a lot had taken place, but despite the diagnosis I knew that God was with me. I knew that there was a purpose for this pit and I had to see this all the way through to the end.

I followed the suggestion of the doctors and had the surgery. The surgery was a success, even though it was very hard on my body. On the day of the surgery I found out that I had a tumor hiding that was the size of a six-month-old baby. The tumor could not be seen through the x-rays. The doctors had to bear witness to the fact that I was very blessed to be alive.

I was very blessed! All that I had been experiencing in my body, mind and spirit was a direct assault and attack on my life from the enemy. But God began to nurture me and visit with me by allowing me to enter a place of praise. I was awestricken by an audience of two.

The more I praised Him, the more I loved Him.

The more I praised Him, the more I adored Him.

The more I praised Him, the more I sought Him, heard Him and believed Him.

The more I praised Him, the more I searched for Him, ran after Him, read about Him and felt Him.

The more I praised Him, the more I needed Him, craved Him, desired Him, cleaved to Him, and wanted Him and nothing else.

The more I praised Him, the more He visited me, revealed His word to me and provided revelation, wisdom, knowledge and counsel.

I fell completely in love again with Jesus but this time it was very different because He truly touched my life in a very powerful way.

I found myself during this horrific sickness drawing closer to the Father like I had never drawn close to Him before. I was put in a situation where if I didn't praise Him I would have died both physically and spiritually.

I was so sick I felt as if I was in a pit with no way of escape. At least this is what the enemy was trying to convince me of. The pain in my body made me feel like I had tasted death.

I thank God today that He had another plan for my life. My praise created a way of escape when there shouldn't have been a way. I like the way Psalms 40:1-3 expresses it, *"I waited patiently and expectantly for The Lord, and He inclined to me and heard my cry. He drew me up out of a horrible pit, a pit of tumult and of destruction, out of the miry clay froth and slime, and set my feet upon a rock, steadying my steps and establishing my goings. And He has put a new song in my mouth, a song of praise to our God. Many shall see and fear revere and worship and put their trust and confidence in The Lord."* Amplified Version

I was determined to stand on the fact that my God is a healer yesterday, today and forevermore. Psalms 26:2 says, *"Prove me, O Lord, and try me, test my heart and my mind."* I had to show God my Job praise, and like Job declare that even though He slay me, yet would I trust Him. During my time of sickness, I could have sulked and threw in the towel. Instead I threw up a PRAISE straight towards heaven. I was intentional about pursuing the presence of God. I ate the word day in and day out. I inhaled the word and I digested it so that I could hide the word in my heart. The more I praised, the better I felt. God's presence became my life stream. What the enemy meant for bad, God was turning it all around to use for His glory so that I could tell His story. It appeared that there was no hope, but I was trusting in the God of hope. Therefore, my flesh may have appeared weak and feeble, but my spirit man was leaping for joy because God was up to something. Jesus touched my broken body and gave me hope again. He put a praise in my mouth that I must and will get out.

"Save me, O God, For the waters have threatened my life [they have come up to my neck]. I have sunk in deep mire, where there is no foothold; I have come into deep waters, where a flood overwhelms me. I am weary, with my crying; my throat is parched. My eyes fail while I wait [with confident expectation] for my God." Psalm 69:1-3, Amplified Version

Due to the severity of the surgery and the impact it had on my body I was on oxygen and I received daily shots to prevent blood clots from forming. I was sent home with a 30-day supply of injections for my stomach. I cried and I screamed with each shot, but it did not prevent me from offering a praise with the same lips. The pits of pain attempted to make me vulnerable. I was feeling hopeless and full of despair and the cares of this life became overwhelming. My pit didn't just start with sickness, but with a broken heart, an ill son, divorce, sick parents, lack of finances and much more. This was a horrible ordeal, but I made it through. The storm left some damage. There were debris all over the place, but in the end God cleaned it all up and today I am here to tell the story. I had to hold on to God and ride this wave all the way to victory. God restored my health to ensure that I would complete my assignments in the earth. He added to my message for others to know that praise will break the bands of sickness.

Chapter Ten

Awakening My Spirit

After returning home from a very difficult and extremely hard surgery, I was faced with months of recovery. Undergoing a Robotic Hysterectomy took a toll on my body and I couldn't stand, walk, shower, or move. I recall crying out to the Lord to take the pain away because it was so unbearable. I received six incisions due to the size of the tumors. However, during my time of recovery, the Lord himself appeared to me and placed a mantle of praising on my life. It was very supernatural and I never understood the importance or power of praise until that time. The Lord Jesus Christ Himself touched my broken, bruised, and battered body and filled me with a strong anointing to praise Him. Not only did He awaken my spirit, mind, and body to praise Him, but His Word became so alive to my inner man, inner personality, and inner conscious. I knew that Jesus had touched me and placed a strong hunger in my spirit to praise Him and to look only to His Word as the source of my Healing. I received a supernatural breakthrough in revelatory knowledge and wisdom. I began to grow strong in the spirit where even on my bed of affliction I would break out in a praise. I would simply praise God with my mouth and the lifting of holy hands. I would read the Word of the Lord and His presence would come upon me and fill my belly. I would feel myself becoming one with the Word, agreeing with the Word and activating the power of the Word in my spirit. The Word of God became so rich in me, that I became a walking and talking spirit. To my amazement my body began to reflect what I was reading and confessing. Although I was in intense pain the Word of God, the Power of The Holy Spirit, and the Supernatural Power of Praise was speaking louder than any pain and trauma that I had been experiencing. It brought a beauty and an assurance that Jesus is truly Lord of my body.

Proverbs 4: 20-22 says, *"My son, attend to my words, consent and submit to my sayings, let*

them not depart from your sight, keep them in the center of your heart, for they are life to those who find them, healing and health to all their flesh."
Amplified Version

The most powerful thing that I learned during my journey of being extremely sick to the point of death, is to never under any circumstance allow the Word of God to depart from my sight. For us to gain victory to receive healing, we must consent to God's Word. *Consent* means to permit, approve, or, agree; it also means to comply and yield. To comply means to act or be in accordance with wishes, request, demands, requirements and conditions of God's Word. To yield means to give up or surrender oneself to God's Holy Word. We must never allow God's Word under any circumstance to depart from our sight. We must always keep the pages of God's Holy, powerful, active and alive Word before us. Doing this will cause you to gain the supernatural ability and creativity needed to keep God's Word in the very center of your heart. The very seed of the Word of God will produce life, health and healing to all your flesh, mind, body, spirit, will, and emotions. As I chose to partner with God and His Word, I gained the supernatural ability and privilege to walk in divine health and healing.

"And the Lord spoke to Moses face to face, as a man speaks to his friend. Moses returned to the camp, but his friend minister Joshua son of Nun, a young man, did not depart from the temporary prayer tent, and Moses said I beseech You, show me Your glory. And God said, I make all my goodness pass before you, and I will proclaim my name The Lord, before you, for I will be gracious to whom I will be gracious, and will show mercy and loving kindness on whom I will show mercy and loving kindness." Exodus 33:11 & 18, 19 Amplified Version

I can truly testify that I met God the Father, God the Son, and God the Holy Spirit face to face during my time of physical affliction. Jesus proved Himself to be more real to me during this time in my life than ever before. I truly knew Him as Savior and Healer. He was real to me and the more I breath in the Word, the Lord truly transformed me. He allowed me the privilege to turn myself completely over to Him through the Beauty of His Presence. His glory rested upon me in a very special way! He showed great mercy and compassion towards me, and the promises of his Word became Alive to Me!

Do you have any idea how God views you through His eyes? I didn't say through the eyes of your mother, your father, your co-workers or pastor, I said through God's eyes. No matter where you are, what you have done, or where you have been your heavenly Fathers deems you beautiful. Yes, we have all sinned, we sin daily, but this does not stop God from loving us. Now let me interject that He loves us as the individual, but He hates the sins that we commit. This is why it is imperative to render praise to a sovereign God who looks past our faults and sees our needs.

I have learned that I don't need man's affirmation of who I am or what I was created to be. My confidence comes from within. It is not about the outer appearance because the word of God declares that true beauty arrives from a gentle and quiet spirit. Therefore, we must allow the lover of our souls to search the hidden treasures of our hearts in order to expose our true beauty. This is the beauty of true praise.

This is a season where the beautiful presence of the Lord is awakening his bride from within. There is an inward cry and fire that is burning from within where the Holy Spirit is positioning His bride to do the unthinkable and achieve the unimaginable. He desires to burn away doubt and unbelief. He does not want His children to experience stress and trauma. He desires to take us to places in the spirit that we have never gone before. A place where we can experience the newness of His presence. In this season, the Holy Spirit desires to melt away pain, sickness and disease, hardship and suffering. Our Father God loves us with a love that is genuine and pure. He desires to heal generations of brokenness and abuse.

He is in touch with our pain and heart break. He knows all who have been abused. He knows about the lonely nights. He knows about that abortion. He is aware of those who are hungry. He is aware of the strife in your life and He knows about your fears. He sees your scars and the hours of the night you are up worrying. He knows about the bills, that you need to feed your kids and that you need a place to stay. He knows about those who slander your name and who gossip behind your back. But there is a hidden beauty that is awakening in this hour. There is an outcry and supernatural birthing of dreams being born and becoming a reality. There is so much glory and beauty of the fragrance of God awakening the bride from within. You will arrive at a beautiful place in the spirit and nothing will be able to pull you from behind the veil. As the

Bride of Christ no one can hinder this heavenly experience with the Father.

In this place, you are able to face your fears head on. You are able to experience the great love He has for you and in return lavish that same love back to Him. In this place, your heartbeat becomes the heartbeat of Christ. Your desires, become His desires and His vision, your vision. You take on the call that has been placed on your life. Jesus is waiting for His bride to climb the stairs of His glory. Allow Him to penetrate the dark places of your life and to exchange them for the very comfort and fabric of His glory. This is truly a season of birthing through and birthing out. It's amazing how our Heavenly bridegroom views us, but he wants us to see ourselves in the same manner that He does, beautiful and lovely. We are His masterpiece, His greatest achievement and most prized possession. We are His greatest glory and we possess the ability to carry His glory within. This glory will take us to places unimaginable and will allow the impossible to become very possible.

Chapter Eleven

Prepared for the Master's Use

I remember the day it felt as if I was dying again. My blood pressure dropped very low and my head began to spin out of control. I was very weak and the pain was unbearable. I was home alone with my son and he had to call the ambulance to rush me back to the hospital. It felt as if the blood was rushing from my body and that I was going into shock. I couldn't do anything but lay there and pray. Again, I was back in the hospital. One night as I was sleeping I saw a dark presence in the form of a woman enter the room. She was either there to make me sicker or to take my life. I immediately began to call on the name of Jesus. As I called the powerful name of Jesus the presence left and I could rest. That night the Lord spoke to me and said that I would live and not die and proclaim the works of the Lord.

I was heavily medicated due to the severity of the pain. I slept for days and hours at a time. The scariest part was battling with dehydration and the low blood pressure at the same time. Again, I was unable to feed myself and I couldn't think straight at all. What hair I had left continued to fall out and didn't know if I was going to see the following day. I couldn't understand why this was happening to me. But even in not understanding, I knew that God was up to something.

It takes great faith to praise your way through the most intimate and difficult circumstances of your life. Faith through praise causes God to release warring angels to fight and intercede on our behalf. There is a supernatural host of angels that tune into this great celebration. As children of God we must become consciously aware of the inner strength that is gained through praise. Many champions have been created through praise. David brought back the Ark of the Covenant through praise. David danced before the Lord and his praise became a sweet-smelling aroma in the nostrils of God. David's praise was sacrificial, therefore he received a supernatural grace. We receive grace when we offer true genuine praise to God. This grace will follow and carry them throughout eternity.

There is something powerful that happens in our spirits when we don't allow ourselves to be conformed to this world or it's superficial customs. *Superficial* means external or outward, concerned with or comprehending only what is on the surface or obvious, shallow, apparent rather than real.

God wants us to understand that the external superficial customs of this world are shallow. These things will fade away. But God wants our minds to be transformed and renewed. I believe we can only have a renewed mind, by stripping off the body of the flesh and its desires and appetites. During my pursuit of praise, I noticed that God was stripping away my old mindset. The filth of the world began to fade away from my life and my presence. I was becoming conformed to the image and likeness of my Savior and things I did even before I became Ill began to fall away from life. Not that I was doing or watching anything bad, but the Spirit of Jesus had come into my life in a fresh new way. The Holy Spirit changed my appetite. I no longer has a desire to watch TV all day, but I desired to sit at the feet of Jesus, presenting myself to Him as a living sacrifice. I knew inwardly that I was different and everything about my life was different as well. I began to view life and myself from Gods perspective. The creator of the universe is pleased when He looks down from Heaven to see His children in hot pursuit of His presence. This is truly an amazing place to be in with Daddy God. Hallelujah!

I remember waking up in the middle of the night with the anointing of the Holy Spirit already upon me. It was a glorious experience! I was being sprinkled clean through the washing of the word of God, and being cleansed by His spirit. Ezekiel 36: 24- 27 declares, *"Then I will sprinkle clean water upon you, and you shall be clean from all your uncleanness and from all your idols will I cleanse you, a new heart heart will I give you and a new spirit will I put within you, and I will take away the stony heart out of your flesh and give you a heart of flesh, and I will put my Spirit with in you and cause you to walk in My statues, and you shall be My people, and I shall be my people, and I shall be your God."* Amplified Version

God was cleansing and purifying me from anything and anyone that would contaminate me and what He was doing inside me. The Lord Himself was preserving me and making me ready for the master's use.

Chapter Twelve

The Call: Go Tell it! The Commission

"But you are a chosen race, a royal priesthood, a consecrated nation, a special people for God's own possession, so that you may proclaim the praises, excellences and the wonderful deeds and virtues of Him who called you out of darkness into His marvelous light." 1st Peter 2:9, Amplified Version

During the fall of 2006 I was experiencing lots of visitations and manifestations that I didn't understand. I knew that it was something special from the Lord, but I couldn't make sense of it all. At the time, I was transitioning out of a church that I had faithfully served for 10 years. I had grown tremendously from a spiritual standpoint during my time there. My Pastors laid a great vocational foundation for me. I had been fully trained in the areas of faith, healing, prayer, redemption, gifts of the Holy Spirit and much more. As I transitioned into the new church I was given an invitation to speak at a ladies' brunch on the morning of September 30, 2006 and I accepted the invitation. During the week of the speaking engagement I said my prayers and I went to bed. As I slept, I began to dream about fire and I began to hear the voice of the enemy ringing loudly in my ears. He said, "If you serve Him I will kill you and everything that you love." I then saw the Lord roll back a rock and speak to me saying, "I am calling you to preach, will you go for me?" I woke up and it felt as if something was choking me because I could not speak. I began to call on the name of Jesus and it lifted. At that moment, I responded to the Lord, with a definite "yes" and He spoke to my heart that He would be with me always.

My response was yes Lord!

"Now the word of the Lord came to me, saying,

"Before I formed you in the womb I knew you [and approved of you as My chosen instrument], And before you were born I consecrated you [to Myself as My own]; I have appointed you as a

prophet to the nations." Then I said, "Ah, Lord God! Behold, I do not know how to speak, For I am [only] a young man." But the Lord said to me,

"Do not say, 'I am [only] a young man, 'Because everywhere I send you, you shall go, And whatever I command you, you shall speak. "Do not be afraid of them [or their hostile faces], For I am with you [always] to protect you and deliver you," says the Lord. Then the Lord stretched out His hand and touched my mouth, and the Lord said to me, "Behold (hear Me), I have put My words in your mouth. "See, I have appointed you this day over the nations and over the kingdoms, to uproot and break down, To destroy and to overthrow, To build and to plant." Jeremiah 1:4-10, Amplified Version

The morning that I was scheduled to minister for the lady's brunch, I was awakened for 5:00am prayer and the Lord revealed Jeremiah 1:4-10 to me.

The brunch was in Marksville, LA and that morning as I was driving to the city the Holy

Ghost came upon me in the car. At that time, I felt a huge burden for the women and the city. When it was my time to minister I began to worship the Lord and I felt the supernatural angelic presence of the Lord. I had never experienced the Holy Spirit in this manner before. As I began to speak my testimony of the goodness of God in my life the Holy Spirit began to illuminate my sight and I could see what each lady was battling with.

The next day was October 1, 2006, it was a Sunday morning and we attended our new church Zion Hill. When we arrived at church worship was highly anointed and packed and I had a strong desire to sit in the back. However, you can't hide from the Holy Ghost. There was a minister speaking under the unction on the Holy Spirit and he and the Pastor of the church were laying hands on people. Once they finished laying hands, the minister grabbed the microphone and began to give a word of knowledge to the Pastor. I was way in the back minding my business and praising God with my hands lifted. Suddenly, the minister called for the lady in the back with the black shirt on. He asked me to quickly run to the front of the church. He said, "You have been arrested by God. You should be dead, sleeping in your grave, but God has chosen you to preach the gospel." He and the Pastor laid hands on me that day. I received the charge from God to preach His word. In January 2007, I received my license to preach and I immediately enrolled in Christ International Bible College. I graduated in May 2012 and I was ordained in 2013. I also attended and graduated from Joy Dara School of Ministry. This is why I praise!

LaChanda's

Pursuit of Praise

Chapter Thirteen

The Effects of Praise

As believer's in Christ praising God must become our greatest need and desire, much like the need to breath. It is truly a gift from God to wake each day with breath in our body, having the activity of our limbs and every need supplied. I didn't want wants, I said needs. But, I have learned that when we praise God and praise from a sincere heart that He will provide both your wants and your needs. I have experienced much turmoil in my life but praise has been my driving force. I refused to stay stuck in bondage when all I have to do is open my mouth. Let me not act as if that is easy for everyone. One of the greatest tricks of the enemy is to get Gods people to be silent and to get them isolated. Our greatest weapon is our praise which requires us to move our lips and to open our mouth and allow sound to break forth. Many times, if we are going through something we tend to sit, ponder and sulk. The more that we sit and ponder, the more leverage the enemy has over us. No, this is the time that if you only have a moan, you moan. If all you can do is yell out the name Jesus, yell until you can't yell anymore. Whatever you do, don't get quiet. God is not moved by your thoughts, He is moved by the sacrifice of your praise.

When I praise God, I become motivated, excited and keen to the things of God. In the same way that He is mindful of me, I become mindful of Him. If I can't praise God, I began to feel stuffy as if my oxygen level is off. When I praise God, it is equivalent to a breath of fresh air. Much like in the beginning when God created male and female, He breathed "puema" which means breath into their nostrils and man became a living being. Amen, I don't know about you, but I desperately need "puema" in my life every day. Especially during the most trying times of my life I am able to inhale God and exhale the deadly toxins that try to invade by body. When I praise God does something new in me each and every time. My praise and worship experiences with God are never the same. This is a time of direct focus on my Father. I take my mind and my eyes off everything around me, place it on the alter and leave it there. This is a beautiful expression of faith. This is a beautiful expression of love between me and my father.

The most indulging gift one can ever imagine, inspired by the Holy Spirit within them to transfer pain into praise. It is authentically praise at its best. It's transforming your sickness into healing, your sorrow into joy, your mourning into dancing, your worship into praise. Your doubting becomes shouting. Your tears become laughter. Your fears become faith. Your helplessness becomes hopefulness. Praising God turns your tragedy into triumphant. Praising God allows you to shift from being the victim to the victor. Praising God brings clear understanding to whose you are and what you are to do. Praising God deepens our intimacy with the Father.

There supernatural substance attracts the blessings and favor of God on our lives. God births and quickens the strong vibrant desire into our spirits to praise Him, because God himself is the creator and giver of praise. Praise is a heavenly language much like praying in the spirit which causes us to become locked into God. We experience God in His purest form when He is lifted high drawing all men unto Him.

Our God is truly a God of the Army of Angels. He comes like lightning to strike all of our foes and leave them shamefully defenseless. As we praise Him He fights for us, He our God contends with those that contend against us. Praising God opens up the gateway to Heaven for us, and it allows us to walk and praise our way right into the very throne room of God. When we enter, the throne room the angels join us and this is an extravagant experience. This is supernatural praise that is effortless, but powerful by defeating spiritual warfare. We must understand Ephesians 6:12 advises us that we wrestle not against flesh and blood, but against principalities, against powers, against the rulers of the darkness of this world, against spiritual wickedness in high places. It is imperative that we grasp hold to the concept that we are fighting a battle that we cannot win in our human frailty. We must have the power of God manifesting in our life through praise. When we find ourselves in spiritual battle we don't have to be defeated because the battle is already won. There are victories won around us seen and unseen everyday as we press into praise with God.

God created you and I by his infinite wisdom, knowledge, and power for the purpose of praise. The power source of love is so extravagant when it comes from the Father of Light that it will cause you to get prostrate before the Lord. The love of our Father is unlike any love that we could ever experience from an earthly human being. This is why I choose to love and adore Him by ministering to Him and about Him. As I write this book I am forever grateful for the presence of God and the Holy Spirit illuminating each word. It is my heart's desire that through this book you will choose a life that is saturated with praise. I have learned through my own personal experience with Jesus that He will not have it no other way. Our Father wants all of us, not part of us, he wants the total package earning, desiring, and thirsting for Him only. He wants us to come into His presence through praise without a sense of guilt or shame attached to us in any ungodly, unholy, and unrighteousness way. When He sees, us He sees us through the cross; through His blood, through his death, burial, and resurrection.

So many choose to believe the lies of the enemy. Yes, we all fall short of Gods glory but God is merciful and forgiving. Therefore, the lies of the enemy cause us to run away from God instead of running to God. Praise will reposition us to find ourselves in a righteous place with God. You don't have to hide from God or feel that God has turned His back on you. He said He would never leave you or forsake you. The love of God covers a multitude of sins. You don't have to feel alone or abandoned. You don't have to feel stressed and depressed. Rise up, open your mouth and declare war on the enemy through praise. Get suited in the Lord and put on your shield of faith knowing that the angels of God are standing with you and have your back. When we do this we put our adversaries to naught ever time. We lift our hands through the purity of our hearts, and the heartbeat of our battle cry and praise God. It doesn't matter what the enemy may throw your way, there is a heavenly solution, you can praise your way through. Hallelujah!!! You can create a miracle in your belly through praise. The following miracles can manifest through your praise:

- Healing
- Deliverance
- Wayward Child Delivered
- Soundness of Mind
- Health and Wellness
- Good Temperament
- Financial Breakthrough
- Relationship Breakthrough

Your miracle of praise can be your birthing place or your birthing position, where you are literally positioning yourself through praise to birth out your miracle. Your miracle through praise may be for an unsaved loved one, where you are engaging in praise for their salvation. Your miracle of praise, can be for healing in your body because the doctors may have giving you a bad report. The doctors may give you days, a week or months to live but God has the last say so. Praise can be a determining factor for moving the heart of God and extended your time on the earth. I know this from personal experience through watching God heal my son Tyrreq as a result of my obedience and praise.

So many times, the enemy attacks us the most in our finances. Marriages are destroyed because of greed or the lack of finances. There are a number of spiritual attacks that result from financial hardship. But you can obtain a miracle of praise where the enemy has snuck in and robbed you of your finances. You can praise your way out of debt into wealth.

Maybe someone has broken your heart and left a whole in your soul. The enemy has attempted to use this to maintain an open wound that is crushing you and causing you to lose focus. You can take comfort and begin to praise based on Psalms 147:3, which says, "He heals the brokenhearted and binds up their wounds." We can bring our brokenness before the Lord like Mary in John 12:3-7. Mary took a pound of ointment of pure liquid nard, a rare perfume that was very expensive, and she poured it on Jesus feet and wiped them with her hair, and the whole house was filled with the fragrance of the perfume.

There is a profound message here. Like Mary you can bring everything that ails you and place it at the feet of Jesus. He will dry your tears and ease your fears. He will cause all trauma to be healed and your broken heart to become like new. He will break every word curse that has been spoken over your life. He will vindicate you for every person that has ever harmed you. He will set you up to bounce back from every set-back and trick of the enemy. He will cause sickness and disease to flee. He will stop the death angel. He will cause generational curses to be uprooted. All this can be done by simply laying your burdens at His feet with praise. You must pour out your love and adoration for him creating an intimate miracle of praise. This will create an alluring aroma that will rise from earth all the way to heaven. Mary was preparing The Lord for his burial and resurrection. And so it is with you, when the enemy has tried to oppress you break the anointing oil through praise and bury the sin, shame, guilt, and fears that have been plaguing your life. You no longer have to accept loneliness, rejection, pain and suffering as your portion. You no longer have to take being abused and mistreated by others. When the enemy tries to use these things to bury your purpose, your gifts, your talents and your destiny there is a higher power who desires to resurrect your life and that higher power is Jesus. He will resurrect your calling, your destiny and your purpose.

Chapter Fourteen

He Made Me Do It: Defining Praise

Serving with gladness is a God given ability and strong desire to serve Him with a grateful heart that is filled with thankfulness. I was once told that you cannot serve the Lord and not fully know and understand if we are pleasing unto Him. God instructed me to take my every day eating, drinking, moving, speaking, and sleeping and offer it as a service unto Him. Through this I had to understand and become fully aware that of His majestic presence. The Lord was teaching me that He was always with me. When we understand that we are always in the presence of God we will seek to serve Him with a spirit of excellence. When we fully understanding that God made us and we did not make ourselves, it gives us a renewed hope and a renewed expectation and a joy to serve. When we serve with a pure heart, there is nothing that God will withhold from His faithful servants. Our Good is a good Father and he desires to lavish

His goodness towards His children in a special way.

I.   **What is Praise?**

- ✓ The state of being approved or admired.
- ✓ To praise someone publicly and enthusiastically.
- ✓ To express approval or admiration of, commend; extol.
- ✓ Praise is the act of expressing approval or admiration, commendation.
- ✓ To offer grateful homage to God or a deity as in words or song.
- ✓ To commend, applaud, express, approval or admiration, to extol inward in song. To magnify and to Glorify God.
- ✓ It is the offering of grateful homage in words or song, as an act of worship, a hymn of praise to God.

The Bible shows that Praise is to be *Declared* or *Manifested*. Praise must function according to our *will, and not our emotions.*

"Judah" Means Praise!

There are three reasons why the lifting of hands is so meaningful when Praising God.

1. We are requesting that God to take us into His arms.
2. We can concentrate on prayer and worship.
3. We make ourselves vulnerable to God. This is very key and very powerful

Vulnerable means that we are standing submissive to God.

Praise must be expressed audibly before others, so that others can benefit from it.

Visible Praise is expressed through dancing, lifting of holy hands, facial expressions, and the Glory of Nature. We must initiate a physical release if we are to experience a spiritual release.

II.   Six Reasons Why We Should Praise the Lord

1. God commands us to Praise Him.
2. God is enthroned in our Praise.

3. There is power in Praise.

4. God is Worthy of our Praise.

5. We were created by God to Praise Him.

6. Praising God is a Good Thing.

III. Entering the Presence of God

There are three manifestations of the Presence of God!

1. His Omniscient Presence.

2. Where two or three are gathered God is in the midst.

3. His Cloud of Glory fills the sanctuary of Praise.

Praise is not so much God coming into our presence as it is our going into His Presence. Hallelujah!! Praise Produces the Presence of God!! When we Praise God, we declare His Kingship, and thus enthrones Him in our Lives. Our responsibility is to Minister to the Lord. According to Psalm 66:2 and, "We should make His Praise Glorious." A sacrifice speaks of something costly and the giving of something that is dear to us. A sacrifice of praise is not a sacrifice until it costs something.

IV.   Three Ways in Which Praise Is Costly

1.   The cost of energy expanded.
2.   The cost of preparation.
3.   The cost of time.

One must prepare yourself by giving themselves to the Word, to prayer and to fasting. Offering upward adoration and exhortations to the Lord by blessing His holy name.

V.   Praise: A Weapon for Spiritual Warfare

The Christian is involved in a spiritual battle, struggle, or war.

Exodus 15:3 declares that, *"The Lord is a man of war."*

2nd Chronicles 20: 1-37, speaks about the battle that was won through praise. Jehoshaphat placed the choir at the head of the army, because he knew the praises would win the Battle.

Warfare through praise does not dictate to God what He should do it, yet it displays praises to Him for His wisdom and might. Praise allows us to recognize that He is capable of handling the problem in the best possible manner.

We are not to focus on the battle or the enemy, we are to look only to the solution. God!! The Problem solver.

VI.   Three Meanings of "High Praise"

1.   A High Level of Intensity.
2.   The Praiser Of Heaven.
3.   Praise that Engages in Spiritual Warfare in Heavenly Places.

Praising, rejoicing and confessing God's sovereignty releases God to fight on our behalf. The sound of Praise is the sound of the Lord bringing retribution upon His enemies which are your enemies. The sound of praise is a sound of war. When we go to war in praise, there is a dimension of faith being released into the atmosphere. By faith we can send our praises like shafts of light, commissioning them to combat in heavenly realms.

VII. Four pitfalls When Attempting Spiritual Warfare Without a Word from God

1. We fight a phantom battle.
2. We might attack brethren.
3. We can miss God's timing.
4. We can attack things God never attended for us to conquer.

VIII. Two Ways to Prepare for Warfare Through Praise

1. By learning to make God's praise Glorious in the time of peace.
2. By feeding on God's Word and Releasing God's word out of our mouth.

God is speaking to His people today because He desires to raise up a Victorious, Conquering, and Overcoming Church that will seek to overcome through praise!

Chapter Fifteen

Praise: The Cure for Rejection

Rejection is the act or state of being rejecting. When we say that someone has a spirit of rejection, it means that the person feels he or she is unloved, unwanted, denied, ignored, and neglected.

The spirit of rejection causes a wound. When one is wounded, many abnormalities take place such as instability in opinion and attitude. Physical ailments can also stem from the spirit of rejection. Rejected individuals can experience heart attacks, hypertension, stroke, mental, emotional and spiritual issues.

Being rejected causes eternal bruises that affects how a person's actions, and how they feel and behave. It causes, extreme stress and trauma and can also lead to depression and oppression. Rejection will cause you to experience cramps and knots in your stomach, which also leads to other serious and sometimes life-threatening sicknesses.

An individual who is being rejected develops a tear in their heart and soul that can only be healed by the power of the Holy Spirit.

It is my belief that rejection stems from a root of bitterness, guilt and shame. When an individual is being rejected the person that is doing the rejecting is more than likely battling with some deep-rooted issues themselves. This individual has no clue how to confront or overcome their issues so they project them upon others. They show very little concern for the feelings of others. The person that is being rejected tends to shy away, withdraw and become isolated. The person that is doing the rejecting will more than likely convince themselves that nothing is wrong with them and everything is wrong with the other person. They fail to realize they are making another person pay for unfair treatment that they received in their lives. Over time this becomes a normal routine and the wounds of the person being rejected and the person doing the rejecting only grows deeper and deeper. Fear can also set in because we desire to be loved by the person rejecting us. The fear stems from our inability to respond to the negative treatment.

Overcoming rejection is possible, but it requires a very deep and intimate relationship with God. It requires being able to forgive self, forgive others and to know that God will never reject His creation. God loves us and He is a God that is always present. Even when Jesus was on the cross and He cried out, "Father, Father, why hast thou forsaken me" we must understand that God did not forsake His Son, but the sin that His Son took on to save you and me. God did not create us to live and dwell in a rejected state. He created us to know and experience love, His agape love. A love that is rich and full of His glory.

I remember being rejected by several people in my life who said they loved me, but there was no real fruit or evidence to prove that love. Even though I experienced this rejection from certain family members, coworkers and church members, I never experienced rejection from my Father. No matter the state I was in, my Father accepted me. During my bouts of rejection, I felt that I had to prove myself to people or better yet gain their approval to be loved. I needed to prove that I was worthy to be a part of their lives without realizing that I didn't have to do that. I was lost and was willing to do whatever I needed to do to be found, but I kept finding myself in a rejected state of being. This began to wear me out and I decided to get before God for His approval of me. I had an experience with God that allowed me to witness the essence and significance of His true love for me. This is why I praise God the way I do, because praise really works.

God has been faithful to His word and has guaranteed His love for me. I was searching for man to love me and accept me when my Creator was always willing without condition. I never needed man's approval, but that is the lie that the enemy feeds you to divert you from having a relationship with God. Psalms 34:8 says, *"O taste and see that the Lord [our God] is good;*

How blessed [fortunate, prosperous, and favored by God] is the man who takes refuge in Him.

Once I tasted the goodness of the Lord and what he had for me, I no longer searched for man to satisfy or complete me. To be honest it got to the point where I began to draw closer to God, with each experience of rejection. This only solidified my relationship with God, making me stronger and preparing me to help deliver others from this tormenting spirit. The following scriptures will help you to understand how much God desires for us to be free in our hearts and in our spirits. Write them upon the tablets of your heart and to dominion over the spirit of rejection. Cast it out in the powerful name of Jesus and watch your life completely turn from night to day.

"Death and life are in the power of the tongue, and those who love it and indulge it will eat its fruit and bear the consequences of their words." Amplified Version, Proverbs 18:21

"A happy heart is good medicine and a cheerful mind works healing, but a broken spirit dries up the bones." Proverbs 17:22, Amplified Version

"A cheerful heart brings a smile to your face; a sad heart makes it hard to get through the day." Proverbs 15:13, The Message

"A healthy spirit conquers adversity, but what can you do when the spirit is crushed?" Proverbs 18:14, The Message

There is a path that has been chosen for each of God's children to travel. If we would follow the course that has been set before us, the chances of us falling into the trap of deception will be rather difficult. God has designed our paths to be filled with blessings and abundance, but that is not to say that there will not be obstacles along the way. He promised that He would make a way of escape. We must recognize the Father's voice and not follow the voice of a stranger. There is a peace, a promise, protection, and provision when we choose to follow the voice of the Lord.

Jeremiah 29:11 says, *"I know what I'm doing, I have it all planned out, plans to take care of you, and not abandon you, plans to give you the future you hope for."* The Message

This is a very familiar passage of scripture, but let us examine it a little closer.

1. We must get out of the way and know that God loves us and that He has wonderful plans for us.
2. He is saying I want my children to live for me, through me, and because of me.
3. He wants us to know how tenderly and compassionately He loves us.
4. He doesn't want us to gain the assurance and the approval from men.
5. He wants us to seek the approval and the assurance of the One who created us.
6. His plan is to gives up a future we always hoped for.
7. Even when we miss the mark the Lord will always be there with open arms ready to

receive and welcome us into His glorious presence.

Jeremiah 29:11, confirms that God has a perfect plan for our lives.

Despite the obstacles and hardships that we face in life, God has a plan. You may have experienced some of the same things I have such as being molested, heartbreak, divorce and sickness but through it all God has a plan. Does He give us all the details of the plans at one time, No! He reveals them in His timing.

Chapter Sixteen

My Mantel & The Altar of Worship

"He said to me, Son of man, eat what you find in this book, eat this scroll, then go and speak to the house of Israel. So, I opened my mouth, and He caused me to eat the scroll. And He said to me, Son of man, eat this scroll that I give you and fill your stomach with it. Then I ate it, and it was as sweet as honey in my mouth. And He said to me. Son of man go, get to the house of Israel and speak to them with my words." Ezekiel 3: 1-4, Amplified Version

It was the summer of 2006 and I had begun to pursue the Lord Jesus Christ and His presence passionately. I had developed an undeniable love for prayer and I would find myself laughing hysterically and wildly in the Holy Spirit. Psalm 16:11 says, *"You will show me the path of life, in Your presence is fullness of joy, at your right hand there pleasures forever."* Amplified Version

One morning during church my Pastor was preaching about faith, and I began to laugh so hard in the spirit that I could not control myself. The Holy Ghost had taken full control of my mouth and spirit and I could not stop laughing. It was evident that I had broken out in the spirit and was experiencing a fountain of the river of God. It was pure life given joy of living water that came from the very throne room of God. It hit my belly and empowered me with a time in His presence that I will never forget. During that time or season in my life I would spend hours and days at a time in prayer. Everything I did was centered around prayer because I was in hot pursuit of the presence and power of God. This was a love for God that I had never experienced in my life. I had such a deep hunger for intercessory prayer. One night after I prayed I fell into a deep refreshing sleep where I saw Jesus Christ Himself walk into the room where I was. He was dressed in a white robe with sandals and He looked remarkable. This was such a surprise to me and to my amazement as I was kneeling to pray,

Jesus himself knelt with me and begin to pray the prayer of intercession with me. He was in total agreement with me and I was in total agreement with Him, and we were in total agreement with God the Father and God the Holy Spirit. This was a very beautiful time with the Lord as He visited with me. He taught me the importance of kneeling to pray to our Father who is in Heaven. I would find myself hungry for the things of God and I could feel the presence of the Holy Spirit prompting me to get away and pray. My son and my husband would often find me hidden away praying to God. My family and friends would come by and call and they would find me praying and having fellowship with my creator. Fasting became a very easy and very natural thing for me as well. In fact, I enjoyed fasting very much, because I became more spiritually conscious or God conscious and it was very easy for me to break out in the spirit and be completed led by the spirit of God. I remember being in my prayer closet one night and praying to God. I was in a place where I was searching for God with all my heart, with all my mind, and with all my strength. The word search means to explore or examine in order to discover, to go or look through a place, area, carefully to find something missing or lost. For me I was in search of a God who was as real to me as my next breath. I was exploring and examining God in my secret place. through worship, the word and staying on my face in my prayer closet or my prayer tent.

Seek means to go in search or quest of, to seek the truth. I was in search of and seeking the truth of who I was, who God was, and ultimately trying to figure out my purpose in the earth. I wanted to know why God created me and who I was to Him. One of the greatest things I discovered during my first season of developing a hunger and thirst for the things of God, was how gentle and loving He was to me. He would sweetly awaken me in the wee hours of the night while everyone else was sleeping to come and have sweet fellowship with me. Many nights, like Paul I would have an outer body experience with the Lord where I would reach the third heavens. I could not tell whether I was in or out of my body, only the Lord knew this for sure.

During these times God began to reveal His heart to me. His desire is for His people to know that He created the trees, seas, forests, mountains and hills to praise. When we see the trees swaying and leaves clapping they are praising the most High God. He created the nations, the lands, man and every living thing to give Him praise. He created the forest and every animal, beast of the forest, and everything that creeps in the forest to give Him praise. He created the birds of the air that fly and mount up close to Him to give Him praise. He also created the rocks to cry out and the oceans mighty waves give Him praise. He created everything that we can see, touch, taste, smell and eat to give Him praise.

LaChanda's

Prophetic Utterances

During the writing of this book God downloaded several prophetic utterances for the Body regarding Praise. Please be open and receptive heeding the voice of the Lord as you read each one. Allow the words to arise from this page and enter your heart where you will cherish each one and allow them to marinate in your soul. Allow these seeds of truth to be implanted in your heart and wait patiently and expectantly for the appointed manifestations of Gods great blessings.

God Speaking to His Body

The days are coming when praise will be the fastest and most profound way to worship. I am raising up a corporate body of believers who truly understand the art and the gift of praising me. I The Lord desire my church to know that it is a privilege and honor to come into the throne room of my presence to praise. This is where I am taking my church, because praise will be the most forceful and anointed way to defeat the Goliath's that are raising war strongly in this hour against the body, my Church. I The Lord am still and will always and forever more be the Supreme Chief Head of my body the church. I am truly looking and expecting my body to overcome and overturn every hidden obstacle and every seen obstacle that may be presented fiercely and fully against them. I have given and impregnated my body with spiritual weapons of warfare to overturn and undo every delay and every set back that they face now in this hour.

The powerful pursuit of praising me and as this pursuit of praising me is taken with my church, you the body are positioning yourselves to trade places with the hosts of Heaven and commissioning the angels of heavens army's to fight for you and on your behalf. All I ask is that you the church give me your Praise!! I The Lord promise that your Praise will offer up to me a sweet-smelling aroma in my nostrils. This type of praise is what gets my attention, keeps my attention, and supernaturally gains my attention. This Praise is a supernatural substance from Heaven that quenches the very fiery darts of the enemy to defeat my body in no way possible. This type of war like praise is possible because it is very unstoppable. What I mean by being unstoppable is when you get thirsty enough to develop and continue praising me in your life, you will begin to sense the nearness of my presence. The peace, power, glory, healing, victory, and anointing that comes from praising me. Then and only then will praising become a priority and not a problem, because once you have tasted and seen the benefits of praising me in spirit and truth and that is a gift from me your Heavenly Father, praising me will be the main course of your daily walking, talking, seeing, breathing, touching, and hearing. Praising me will become your all and all, because you know in your heart of hearts that praising me your Lord and savior is what truly satisfies me. I am moved with great compassion on the man, woman, teenager, or child who chooses to praise rather than chooses to worry. I said in my word time and time again praising me is truly a powerful weapon that diffuses and nullifies all the forces of darkness. As spoken in my most holy word, *"Let everything that has breath Praise The Lord*!! Psalm 150: 6

Praise Declaration

My Praise Is a Weapon, yes, it's a Declaration, if God be for me, tell me who can be against me and no weapon from the enemy shall prosper. I Praise Him! I Praise Him! I Lift Him High!

Praising me is your way of truly expressing your love for me. One cannot truly express their love for me without giving me praise. Remember I created everything with the awareness of giving me praise. I understand praise because I am the creator and maintainer of it. I created rocks, trees, birds, the seas, everything in the seas, the lands, everything that creeps and crawls on the lands, the heavens, angels and everything in the heavens to praise me. I created the earth and sky and everything that flies in the sky to praise me. I created instruments to give me praise, and most importantly I created you to give me the praise. I created you with hands, feet, and lips to give me praise and to live your life for the Praise of My Glory!!

"But you are a Chosen race, a royal Priesthood, a Consecrated Nation, a special people for God's own Possession, so that you may proclaim the excellences, the wonderful deeds and virtues and perfections of a Him who called you out of darkness into His marvelous light." 1st Peter 2:9

I Am the Most High God

I want my people to know that I am a God who hears and listens. I am also God who loves every one of my children in a very special and unique way. No one fully understands the deep secrets, deep emotions, deep feelings or deep concern and compassion that I have for my beloved children, who are mine. Those in whom I have called and chosen by name and to live out their precious lives for the Praise of My Glory Only! I want my beloved children to know that I their Lord am sitting in the Heavens, the Holy of Holies watching over and keeping watch over my precious creation in whom I have formed for myself, because I love them. I want my children to know that I their Lord have released my heavenly angels over them to protect them, especially as they are obeying and releasing my Holy Word out of the fruit of their mouth. As they come into agreement with me and my Holy Word, angels of heavens armies are being released and sent out for the service of my people to dismantle all the forces of darkness from prevailing against them. I want my beloved children to know that I am releasing a special richness of my spirit on them in this hour. This great richness of my glory and my power will overshadow a great host of my children as it did my servant Mary, when the Angel Gabrielle appeared to her and spoke that she would become impregnated with a son. He would be the Savior of the world and that the seed she would be carrying would be holy, consecrated, and set apart by God and for God alone. His name would be Jesus and he would save my people from their sins. I The Lord am speaking in this hour to my children, that the holy angels of God will begin to visit with them and give strategic plans and assignments that come from Me. I am unlocking gifting's, talents, and Holy Ghost abilities that come directly from my Holy presence as my children yield to me with a holy response. Let it be according to My will, plan, and purpose for your life. I want my children to know that is what attracts my attention and propels me to do more for my children, more than they can think of, wish for, hope for, dream of, image, ask for, according to my Holy Ghost power that is supernaturally working in them. Just as there was an awakening of my spirit in Mary the mother of Jesus, so should there be like never before an awakening in the spirit within my children. They should be burning inwardly with a strong and deep sense of my holy presence igniting them with the freshness of the winds of my holy presence. They will carry my message of faith, hope, and love to a lost and dying generation. Says the Lord!

Dear Church

Thus, says the Lord of host. It gives me a privilege and honor to know that so many of my children are hungering and thirsting for me in a deeper way. Your Lord says when you search for Me with all your heart, mind, and soul, I the Lord will be found by you. When you draw closer to Me, I will draw closer to you, and I will consume you and we will be partners for life unto eternity.

It saddens me also to know that so many of my children are not seeking the things of God, nor the things of my Kingdom. Don't you know I am the Almighty God, and there is no lack of anything you may need or desire in Me! I the Lord am all you need. But first you must trust Me and the awesome ability of My power. State your case! Let us plead together and see won't I make a way out of the wilderness for you My beloved children. I am the true and living GOD and besides Me there is no other. I your Father longs and desire to know you in a fuller, deeper, and more intimate way, but first you must come to me. Summit and surrender your all to me and when I say all I mean all. For My yoke is easy and My burden is light and easy to bare. I am He who pulled you out of your mother's womb and breathed My very life, the breath of my life into your nostrils. I your Lord I am the very Fountain of Life, I am life itself. For I the Lord carried you in my bosom, created you from the dust of the ground. To be greatest in my heavenly kingdom, I knew you before the world, I fashioned and formed you in My own image, to live for the praise of My glory. Therefore, you are fearfully and wonderfully made. Don't be afraid of Me but come to Me out of obedience to who I am and what I can do to you, in you, among you and for you. Don't you know I am a GOD who is more than enough, didn't I tell you I will never leave you nor forsake you, no not never, you are my sheep and I take great care of my sheep. You must allow me to, stop going to and for asking people of this world for things and ask me. Didn't I say I would do exceedingly, abundantly, far over and above all you may dare ask, think, imagine, dream, pray, hope, or desire according to the Holy Ghost power that worketh in you. My children run your race and run your race well that is set before you, and I your Lord and Savior Jesus Christ I promise you, my beloved children, you will all receive the Victor's Crown of Glory. But first you must empty yourself out, so I can fill you up. Fill you with my power, my wisdom, my knowledge, my insight, my revelation, my discernment, my interpretation into spiritual matters, my intelligence, my glory, my understanding, and my anointing. You may truly begin to trust Me and the works that I do, and the greater works that I desire to do through you my beloved children. My works are sure, confident, faithful, trustworthy, reliable, dependable, desirable, teachable, assessable, acknowledgeable, done in true excellence, and with the power of my immeasurable, love, grace, and demonstrated and manifested in the completeness of my very own authority that rest so richly on you my beloved children. I have said and spoken it, and

I will do just as I have promised in My word I will do. I have proclaimed it and I will make it good. I am your Father and I Love you the way only a true Father can love His beloved children. But I ask that you love Me back the same exact way, and you'll see My glory, my grace, my mercy, my love, and my unmerited favor begin to arise in your life. Come now and I will wash you, sanctify you, cleanse you, separate you, consecrate you, and make you whole and holy, if you are willing and obedient you will eat the good of my land. Love Your Heavenly Father

A Time to Shout

A Sound of Triumph! A Sound of Victory!

"But thanks be to God, who in Christ always leads us in triumph, as trophies of Christ's victory and through us spreads and makes evident the fragrance of the knowledge of God everywhere."
2nd Corinthians 2:14, Amplified Version

There is a is sound of heavenly triumph and there is a sound of great victory when my people come and join themselves corporately and individually with me. As they begin to join the forces of Heaven to bring me Glory and Praise, there is a triumphant heavenly charge in the atmosphere of Heaven. This brings great victory in the earth realm that captures My heart. As you partner with the angelic host of Heaven to bring forth this beautiful heavenly sound, the atmosphere of Heaven begins to shift on your behalf in the heavens and there upon the earth. There is a supernatural charge of My holy presence that unlocks the realm of the spirit that will bring forth supernatural heavenly joy and rejoicing. Praising me is the serious business of Heaven. My people through praise gain more territory, win many battles, defeat many giants, and overcome many obstacles through the ongoing supernatural power of praise. There is a supernatural supply of My Holy Ghost power that is released in the heavens unto the earth, that will fill my people with so much joy in believing, because praising me attracts the blessings of the Lord upon your life. This supply of the spirit of praise, will supernaturally pull my people out of the deepest pits of despair, fear, rejection, setbacks, sickness, disease and failure. Praise will cause my people to trust in me as the living God, because I will demonstrate the greatness of my power through praise. I the Lord will baptize my people with the baptism of praise. This is the reason I created the mouth, hands, and feet, so my people can give back to me the beautiful aroma of praise which is a sweet-smelling aroma in my nostrils. Says the Lord! I like to call it a beautiful exchange of My power and glory into the hearts, spirits, minds, souls, and the body of My people, who have been called and chosen by Me.

This sound of praise will cause the wall of Jericho to come down when people march around the great mountains in their life seven times. This sound of praise will reverse the curse of cancer. This sound of praise will reverse lupus, asthma, diabetics, lack, failure, unbelief and loneliness. When my people praise me I inhabitant the praises of my people. This sound of praise pulls my people out of the pits of darkness and brings them into my marvelous and glorious light. Says the Lord!

Praise Declaration Song

Praise Him in The Morning!

Praise Him in The Noonday!

Praise Him in The Evening!

Praise Him in The Midnight Hour!

Praise Him When You're Happy!

Praise Him When Your Sad!

When Praises Go Up It Makes the Devil Mad!

Praise Him! Praise Him! Praise Him! Praise Him!

Praise Him! Praise Him! Praise Him!

Scriptures to Meditate On

The Lord is close to those who are of a broken heart and saves as are the crunched with sorrow for sin and are humbly and thoroughly penitent. Amplified Version, Psalms 34:18

My flesh and my heart may fail, but God is the Rock and firm strength and my Portion forever. Amplified Version, Psalms 73:26

Cast your burden on The Lord (releasing the weight of it and He will sustain you, He will never allow the consistently righteous to be moved, made to slip, fall or fail). Amplified Version, Psalms 55:22

Heals the broken hearted and binds up their wounds, curing their pains and their sorrows. Amplified Version, Psalms 147:3

Fear not, there is nothing to fear, for I am with, do not look around you in terror and be dismayed, for I am your God. I will strengthen and harden

you to difficulties, yes, I will help you, yes, I will hold you up and retain you with My victorious right hand of rightness and justice. Amplified Version, Isaiah 41:10

He sends forth His word and heals them and rescues the from the pit and destruction. Amplified Version, Psalms 107:20

Come to Me, all you who labor and are heavy-laden and overburden, and I will cause you to rest. I will ease and relieve and refresh your souls. Amplified Version, Matthew 11:28-30

Ascribe to The Lord the glory due His name. Bring an offering and come before Him; worship The Lord in the beauty of holiness and in holy array. Tremble and reverently fear before Him, all the earth's people, the world also shall be established, so it cannot be moved. Let the heavens be glad and let the earth rejoice, and let men say among the nations. The Lord reigns! Let the sea roar, and all things that fill it, let the fields rejoice, and all that is in them, Then shall the trees of the wood sing out for joy before the presence of The Lord, for He comes to judge and govern the earth. O give thanks to The Lord, for He is good, for His mercy and loving-kindness endure forever! And say, Save us, O God of our salvation, gather us together and deliver us from the nations, that we may give thanks to your holy name and glory in Your praise. 1st Chronicles 16: 29-35, Amplified Version

Sing, O ye heavens; for The Lord hath done it, shout ye lower parts of the earth; break forth into singing, ye mountains, O forests, and every tree therein, for The Lord hath redeemed Jacob, and glorified himself in Israel. Isaiah 44:23, Amplified Version

For ye shall go out with joy, and be led forth with peace, the mountains, and the hills shall break forth before you into singing, and all the trees of the field shall clap their hands. Isaiah 55:12, Amplified Version

Let the heavens rejoice, and let the earth be glad, let the sea roar, and the fullness thereof. Let the field be joyful, and all that is therein, then shall all the trees of the wood rejoice.) Psalm 96: 11-12, King James Version

About the Author

LaChanda Sumbler is

a compassionate Pastor, Evangelist, preacher and teacher of the good news of the gospel. Her passion is winning souls and seeing the body of Christ come into the saving knowledge of Jesus. She carries an anointed healing and prophetic mantle upon her life. The Lord Jesus Christ has truly graced and anointed LaChanda to impart His healing power to every woman she encounters. LaChanda is the founder of "Life In The Word Ministries" and "Women Living With Purpose Ministries." LaChanda is a loving mother to her 19-year-old son Tyrreq.

For bookings and speaking engagements please visit www.mypursuitofpraise.org or contact 318-542-6731 or via email lsumbler74@gmail.com or mypursuitofpraise@gmail.com.